Windows® CE

Clear & Simple

Windows® CE
Clear & Simple

Craig Peacock

BOSTON OXFORD AUCKLAND JOHANNESBURG MELBOURNE NEW DELHI

℞ Butterworth–Heinemann is a member of the Reed Elsevier Group

 Recognizing the importance of preserving what has been written, Butterworth–Heinemann prints its books on acid-free paper whenever possible.

 Butterworth-Heinemann supports the efforts of American Forests and the Global ReLeaf program in its campaign for the betterment of trees, forests and our environment.

Library of Congress Cataloging-in-Publication Data

Peacock, Craig, 1969–
    Windows CE clear & simple / Craig Peacock
        p.   cm.
    ISBN 0-7506-7232-3 (alk. paper)
    1. Microsoft Windows (Computer file) 2. Operating systems
(Computers) I. Title. II. Title: Windows CD clear & simple
QA76.76.063P434 1999
    005.4'469—dc21   99–39644
                                                                  CIP

British Library Cataloguing-in-Publication Data
A catalogue record for this book is available from the British Library

The publisher offers discounts on bulk orders of this book. For information, please write:
Manager of Special Sales
Butterworth–Heinemann
225 Wildwood Avenue
Woburn, MA 01801–2041
Tel: 781-904-2500
Fax: 781-904-2620

For information on all Butterworth-Heinemann publications available, contact our World Wide Web home pages at: http://www.bh.com

10 9 8 7 6 5 4 3 2 1

Printed in the United States of America
Composition: 🖋 P.K.McBride, Southampton
Icons designed by Sarah Ward © 1994

Contents

Foreword

Many of the studies conducted by market research firms of the lifestyles of men and women today show a sense that time is the most precious commodity, more valuable than money or possessions. The escalating demands of the workplace and other chores leave little time for couples to spend with one another, for family activities, or even time to enjoy a book or music. "If only there were a way to create more time without sacrificing commitments and responsibilities," they say.

The pressures of modern life have caused some people to complain of short-term memory loss. Some try to cope by carrying paper planners stuffed with all sorts of documents and scraps of paper. Some people manage very well with paper, others complain that it is all too much. The diversity of paper calendar systems is breathtaking. One recent survey indicated that the average price paid for a paper calendar was $14, yet the sales of all paper calendars tracked by the survey numbered into the billions of dollars.

From the first introduction of the personal computer until today's Pentium III-based powerhouses, companies began to apply the power of the computer to the classic time management and information organization problem. Personal Information Management software for the PC has evolved a great deal over the years, with almost as many options as the humble paper calendar, while sales of PIM software are much less than the paper calendar.

One reason why PIM software has not surpassed paper is the innate portability and convenience that paper provides. A blank sheet of paper is the most fungible of all materials; it can become any document the author wishes. There is no "boot time" for paper, and it is only somewhat more susceptible to damage from water or fire than a PC.

For more than a decade, companies have been working on a concept to marry the benefits of paper to the power of the computer. Today's Windows CE-based Handheld PCs (H/PC) and Palm-size PCs (P/PC) are the latest examples of that effort. Thousands of people at dozens and dozens of companies have brought these products forth, from the manufacturer, to software and hardware developers, even companies that manufacture custom cases for your device of choice. Together with Microsoft, these companies are bringing a new industry together to provide solutions for the time and information management problems we all share.

Still, the H/PC and P/PC are tools that can be wielded for maximum benefit if you have a guide to help you learn the basics, uncover the full potential of the device, and apply the tools and knowledge to customize a solution for your unique needs. I'm a member of the team that works on the tools, and it is my pleasure to introduce you to your guide, Craig Peacock, who will lead you on to a better understanding of how to use the tools to help you regain part of your life for yourself again.

Enjoy the journey.

Jim Floyd

Product Manager, Windows CE Marketing, Microsoft Corp.

Preface

This book starts off by introducing the different hardware platforms that run Windows CE. Handheld PCs, Palm-size PCs and the Handheld PC Professional machines are all covered. Throughout the book you will see step-by-step instructions for all the main Windows CE and third party applications that handle the commonly performed tasks you may want to do on your Windows CE mobile device. Tips and notes are provided throughout the book to help you get the most out of whichever type of Windows CE device you own.

Most of the applications are available on all three devices, and so the steps to perform any task are almost identical. As you will see in the section showing the differences between the devices, it's mainly the screen sizes that are radically different – the applications still retain that Windows look and feel and perform the same functions.

If you are thinking of using Windows CE or are an existing user, then you will, I hope, find this book equally useful.

This book would not have been possible without the incredible levels of assistance given to me by some of the folks at Microsoft and the staff from other vendors who gave me access to product information months before it was due to be released. So many people have helped me with this project and I thank you all.

Lily, my love, to you for having the patience to put up with me spending all those hours in front of those *"damn computers!"*

My thanks go to the following people all of whom have exceptionally busy jobs and yet still found time to help me. My sincere thanks to Jim Floyd for giving me the inspiration to go for it and for instilling me with the enthusiasm for Windows CE several years ago, Neil Enns for helping me in the critical final stages. Neil, you opened doors where I thought only walls existed – your timely responses to my questions helped me to get the book finished. Richard Brown for sharing your thoughts on Windows CE and helping me with the tough bits! Jason Nottingham for teaching me that the light switch at the end of the tunnel is sometimes hidden. Jason also wrote the program to capture some of the images seen in this book for which I am exceptionally grateful. My friends and fellow Windows CE enthusiasts Kieren Spooner, Fraser Larcombe, John O'Donnell, Dan Hantulla, Todd Ogasawara and John Kennedy, your friendship and professional guidance helped me navigate the path to completion of this book.

I'd like to thank the people that started me off on my quest to help make Windows CE Made Simple – the visitors to my Web site. If it wasn't for the hundreds of e-mails I received every day asking for all sorts of help on Windows CE, I wouldn't have realized the opportunity and written this book.

All the folks at Butterworth-Heinemann have given me lots of help and support during the course of this project, especially Peter McBride, Mike Cash, Catherine Fear and Derek Brown.

Above all I hope you find this book useful. It is packed full of little tips and tricks which I hope will make your use of Windows CE easier and more efficient.

Craig Peacock, 1999

1 Start here

Introducing Windows CE

Windows CE is available on devices called Handheld PCs, Palm-size PCs and Auto PCs. In this book I will cover the Handheld, Handheld Pro and Palm-size devices and I'll refer to all three types of machines as mobile devices. I will show you how to get the most out of the Handheld PC and Palm-size platforms and illustrate the differences and similarities of the two platforms in this chapter. This book covers both Windows CE 2 and Windows CE 3.0.

It is possible to have lots of applications open at the same time on Windows CE and on the Palm-size PC you never actually have to shut down any applications. If this sounds a little strange, it will all become much clearer later in this chapter.

What is Windows CE?

Windows CE is one of the newest members of the Windows family. It enables a large and varied number of electronic devices to run Windows. It has been an amazing success and it promises to revolutionize the way people carry information around with them. This exciting new platform from Microsoft has, for the first time, enabled people to have access to the information they normally keep on the desktop PCs and on their corporate networks in the palm of their hand, where they need it.

Windows CE has the look and feel of the Windows operating system you use on your PC. It is not just Windows made smaller, but has been designed from scratch to include some of the best features of the desktop operating systems and to provide a few new firsts. Instant on and touch-sensitive screens are two of my favorite Windows CE features.

Take note

One feature of Windows CE that is present due to the smaller screens (smaller than your desktop PC's Screen) is that you can only have one window maximized at any one time. There is no concept of overlapping windows or of resizing windows to allow several to be displayed at once.

Tip

To get the start menu up, tap the button labeled "Start" with your stylus, it is in the bottom left-hand corner of the screen on your mobile device.

Features of Windows CE

Windows CE integrates with your desktop Windows PC seamlessly and if you've recorded information, whether it be a name and address, a phone number, a business report or even a voice recorded note you can transfer that information to your PC without the need to retype or reenter it. Windows CE saves you time and effort. With Windows CE you can quickly and easily find information that's stored electronically.

One of the main strengths of Windows CE is the synchronization it allows with your desktop computer. Frequently changing information such as appointments, tasks and contacts details are where this synchronization shows up best.

Instant on – when you switch on your computer it instantly comes on. If you leave 5 applications open and switch off the device, the next time you switch it on, all your applications are still open and all your data is still there. It's a feature you'll wish you had on your desktop PC.

Battery life – Handheld PCs and Palm-size PCs have been designed with good battery life in mind. You should get more than 8 hours' constant use from a Handheld PC and more than 20 hours' use from a Palm-size PC. (All manufacturers' details vary. These are approximate values taken from my use of many different devices.) In comparison, you'll find that many laptops these days have batteries that last only 2 or 3 hours.

Handheld or **Palm-size** – it fits in my hand, so is it a Handheld PC or a Palm-size PC? In the section on the differences you'll see what makes a Handheld PC different from a Palm-size PC.

Memory Size – The amount of memory shipped in each device varies from 4Mb up to 32Mb

The differences

Handheld, Handheld Pro and Palm-size PCs run very similar software. The biggest difference between them is in their size. Palm-size PCs are the smallest of all Windows CE devices and are able to fit into a pocket. Handheld PCs are slightly larger and feature a 640x240 ½ VGA screen. The largest devices running the Handheld PC Professional operating system typically have full VGA screens, with resolutions of 640x480 or higher.

Handheld PCs have a physical keyboard and this, along with the larger screen allows people to be a little more creative. Palm-size PCs do not have a keyboard. Instead, they have the *SIP* – Software Input Panel – which provides a software keyboard and handwriting recognition (see Chapter 2). This is only one of the methods that you can get data into your Palm-size PC. Another major feature of the Palm-size PCs is a Voice Recorder, which can be activated without even switching the machine on.

You won't find Microsoft Pocket Word, Pocket Excel or Pocket Powerpoint on the Palm-size PCs, but you will find them as standard on the Handheld PC.

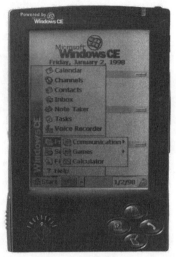

Palm-size PC

Handheld PC

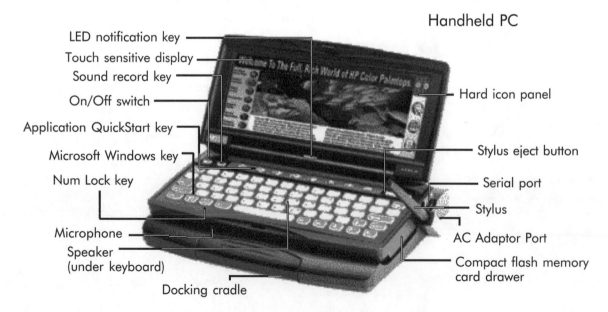

LED notification key
Touch sensitive display
Sound record key
On/Off switch
Application QuickStart key
Microsoft Windows key
Num Lock key
Microphone
Speaker (under keyboard)
Docking cradle

Hard icon panel
Stylus eject button
Serial port
Stylus
AC Adaptor Port
Compact flash memory card drawer

Some hardware vendors bundle third-party software with their products. This table only shows the standard Microsoft applications supplied on these machines.

Application	Handheld PC Pro	Handheld PC	Palm-size PC
ActiveSync	*	*	*
Calculator	*	*	*
Calendar	*	*	*
Contacts	*	*	*
Pocket Access	*		
Pocket Excel	*	*	
Pocket Word	*	*	
Inbox	*	*	*
Inkwriter	*		
Internet Explorer	*	*	
Mobile Channels	*		*
Note Taker			*
Pocket PowerPoint	*	*	
Solitaire	*	*	*
Tasks	*	*	*
Voice Recorder	*	*	*
World Clock	*	*	*

Handheld PC Pro

Take note

Microsoft has released a Mobile Channel Viewer for the Handheld PC and Handheld PC Pro. For more details on this, visit the Microsoft Web Site at:
http://www.microsoft.com

Handheld PC screen

When you first see Windows CE on the Handheld PC you'll be presented with the screen at the bottom of this page. It's known as the Startup Screen and also the Desktop.

Note the **Start** button, as this is how you'll navigate and run applications on your Handheld PC.

Icons – click on these to start applications

Desktop Area – you can change the background and create shortcuts to run your favorite applications quickly

Return to Desktop button – tap to go back to the desktop screen

Start Button – opens the Start menu to run programs, access recently used documents, get help and change settings

Taskbar – when an application is running, its title is displayed here

Take note

The Handheld PC screenshots in this book are from an **HP 620 LX**. With over 20 Windows CE machines on the market, your screen may look a little different, but the changes should be minimal as Windows CE is the operating system running on all of them.

Palm-size PC screen

Tip

The Help system on mobile devices works in the same way as on desktop PCs, except that it is context-sensitive. Tap Start – Help from any application, and the Help that you are offered will be relevant to the job in hand at the time.

Palm-size PCs also run Microsoft Windows CE, but there are differences.

The Palm-size startup screen is referred to as the Active Desktop, this is because all is not as it first appears. Shown here are details of the owner, upcoming appointments and active tasks, but all of this can be changed by the user.

To access your Appointments or Tasks, double-tap on the Title Bar for that application.

With the collapsible Indicator, you can resize the display, so if you want to have more room showing your appointments or tasks, drag the icon up or down the screen to resize that area.

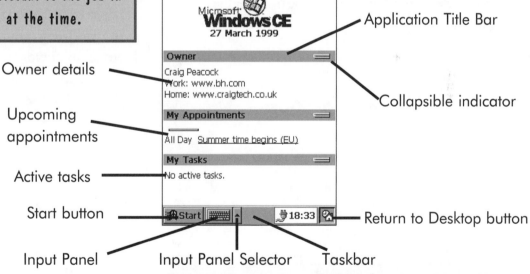

Owner details

Upcoming appointments

Active tasks

Start button

Input Panel

Application Title Bar

Collapsible indicator

Return to Desktop button

Input Panel Selector   Taskbar

Take note

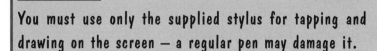

You must use only the supplied stylus for tapping and drawing on the screen – a regular pen may damage it.

The Palm-size PC shown on page 7 offers a familiar interface to all recent Microsoft Windows products, has a start menu in the bottom left-hand corner of the screen, but with the start menu "minimized" the differences begin to show up.

- **Start Button** – Use this to find and run programs, access recently-used documents, get Help and change settings on your Palm-size PC.

- **Active Desktop** – Various pieces of information can be displayed here so you can see things quickly. As standard this is the Owner information, Appointments for today and Active Tasks. In the next section you will find out how to customize the Active Desktop.

- **Application Title Bar** – Shows the name of the application that is displayed on this part of the Active Desktop.

- **Owner information** – This will have your name and phone numbers displayed.

- **Upcoming Appointments for Today** – Lists today's appointments.

- **Active Tasks** – List any tasks due today.

- **Collapsible / Slider bar** – This icon tells you that you can move the section up or down – have a try. Press and hold with the stylus and move it up or down.

- **Input Panel** – With a Palm-size PC there are several ways to enter data. The Input Panel shows you which one is currently selected.

- **Input Panel Selector** – To change the type of input method, tap this arrow and make your selection.

- **Return to Desktop button** – When you are in any application tap this to return to the Desktop.

Touch-sensitive screen

All Windows CE devices have a touch-sensitive screen, and if you tap this with the special stylus the system will respond.

On a desktop PC you would have a cursor displayed on the screen and when this cursor is over a particular application or piece of text you would use your mouse to click and double-click for it to perform various actions. On Windows CE there is no cursor and to have the same effect you tap the part of the screen directly with the stylus.

Data entry

The two standard input methods on these devices are handwriting recognition and the on-screen keyboard. Several third-party companies produce other input methods and panels for these devices.

Running applications

❏ To start an application

1 Double-tap an icon.

Or

2 Tap Start and select from the menu.

❏ To see the Desktop

3 Tap the Return to Desktop icon in the lower right-hand corner of the screen.

Or

4 Minimize the application by tapping its Taskbar button.

On the Handheld PC you can either start the applications by "double-tapping" on a desktop icon or using the Start menu.

The Taskbar shows you which applications you have open, and enables you to bring up applications that are running very quickly. Windows CE is a multitasking operating system, which means you can have multiple applications open at the same time and quickly and efficiently switch between them.

Maximize and minimize

You can only have one window maximized (filling the whole screen) at any time. Any others are minimized to buttons on the Taskbar. Tap on a Taskbar button to maximize its application; tapping it a second time will minimize the application again.

1 Double-tap an icon

2 Tap Start and select from the menu

3 Tap Return to Desktop

4 Tap its Taskbar button

Above: Pocket Word, Excel and 8 applications are running, but minimized onto the Taskbar

Installing software

When you want to install a new software package on your Windows CE device, the procedure is almost identical to that of installing software on a PC.

The software is usually supplied either over the Internet or on a diskette or CD-ROM and it will have a setup.exe file that you need to run on your PC. Running this setup.exe file will then copy the application to the Windows CE device. The device must, of course, be connected to the PC before you start installation.

When the software is copied to your device it will add an entry in the Start menu system.

These screen shots are taken from a PC, the procedure for installing software is identical on all Windows CE devices.

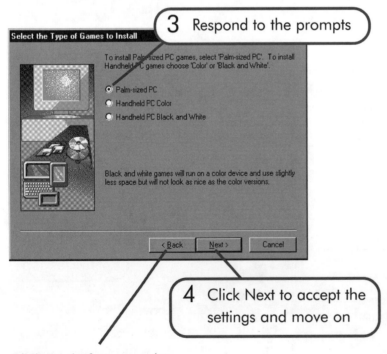

3 Respond to the prompts

4 Click Next to accept the settings and move on

Click Back if you need to change an earlier choice

Basic steps

1 Connect your CE device up to your PC.

❑ On your desktop PC

2 Run the application's setup.exe program, by double clicking on it on your PC.

3 The setup software might prompt you for information of choices. You might be asked the type of device you have or, if the package has various parts, which components you want to install.

4 After completing each panel, click the Next button, then Finish at the last panel.

5 Click Yes to confirm the installation, then wait while files are copied across.

6 Click OK at the end then check your device screen to see if further steps are needed to complete the setup.

If there are optional
components, tick those
that you want to install

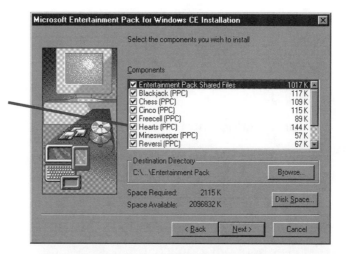

Tip

If you are not sure which
choices to make, accept
the default settings —
they are usually the best
for new users.

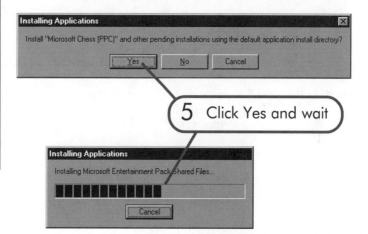

5 Click Yes and wait

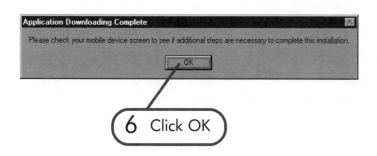

6 Click OK

Tip

Take the usual precautions of
making sure the files are from
a known source before installing any new software on your PC
or your Windows CE device.

Summary

- ❑ Windows CE runs on different size machines called Handheld PCs and Palm-size PCs.

- ❑ The Startup screen on each device has different characteristics.

- ❑ Use the Start menu to find the applications you want to run.

- ❑ You can resize parts of the Active Desktop on the Palm-size PCs.

- ❑ Use the context-sensitive online Help to find out more details about any application.

- ❑ There are different applications on Handheld PCs and Palm-size PCs.

- ❑ On the Handheld PC you can launch applications by double-tapping on the icons on the desktop.

- ❑ You can run multiple applications at the same time.

- ❑ New software is installed onto a mobile device through a connected PC.

2 Setting up

Localizing Windows CE

When you first set up your Windows CE device, a Wizard will take you through various settings such as which country you live in and the time and date.

The settings are changed through the Control Panel on the Handheld PCs and from the Settings menu of Palm-size PCs.

❑ Palm-size PCs

1 Tap Start.

2 Tap Settings.

3 Tap Regional Settings.

❑ Handheld PCs

4 Tap Start.

5 Tap Settings.

6 Tap Control Panel.

7 Double-tap the icon for Regional Settings.

Palm-size PC

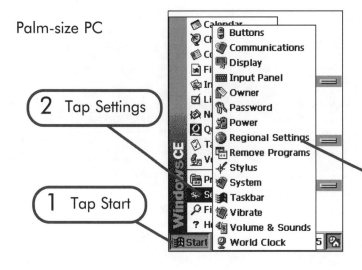

2 Tap Settings

1 Tap Start

3 Tap Regional Settings

Handheld PC

7 Double-tap the icon

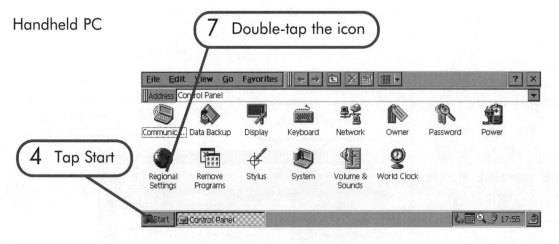

4 Tap Start

Basic steps

❑ Language

1 Tap the drop-down box in the bottom right-hand corner.

2 Type the first letter of your language or use the arrow keys to find the correct one.

❑ Number display

3 Tap the Number tab at the top of the panel.

4 Set the number format as required.

Tip

Don't click the OK button until you have worked through all the panels. When you click it, the dialog box will close.

Regional Settings

In the Regional Settings section you will see five screens with various options – Regional Settings, Number, Currency, Time and Date. You may well find you only wish to change one or two of the defaults.

The key settings is the country – this affects many of the other settings.

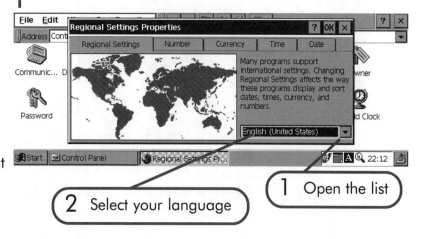

2 Select your language

1 Open the list

Number

If you like to have the numbers represented in a certain way, such as displaying negative numbers in brackets, e.g., (30) rather than -30, or if you prefer to have 4 digits after the decimal place, then this is where you would make those changes.

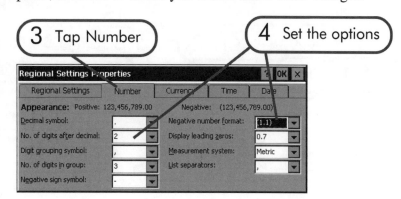

3 Tap Number

4 Set the options

Currency

The settings on this panel are very similar to those for numbers. Select the currency symbol and set other options as required.

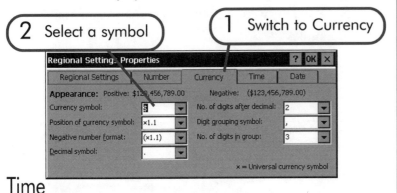

Time

Use the time settings to format the time display in the Taskbar.

The sample
shows how
it will look

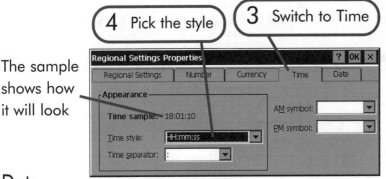

Date

There are several date formats; here it is shown as day/month/year. Both the format and the date separator can be changed.

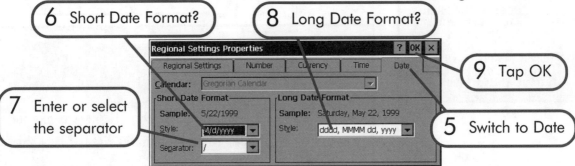

Basic steps

❑ Currency

1 Switch to Currency.

2 Select the symbol.

❑ Time

3 Switch to the Time tab.

4 Tap the Time style: drop-down arrow and select either 12 or 24 hour clock formats.

❑ Date

5 Switch to the Date tab.

6 Select a Short Date Format.

7 Tap the Separator field and enter the character or select one from the list.

8 Select a Long Date Format.

9 Tap OK to save your settings and exit.

Basic steps

❑ Starting Contacts

1 Tap Start – Programs and select Pocket Outlook.

2 Tap Contacts.

❑ Country and area code

3 Tap Tools.

4 Tap Options...

5 Select the Country.

6 Enter a default Area Code if required.

7 Tap OK.

Localizing Contacts

In the Contacts application there are a couple of fields that are country/area specific; this is where you can change the defaults which are entered for you when you create a new contact. These can, of course, be overwritten, but if you have a lot of contacts in the same country or area code, setting these as the defaults will save time later.

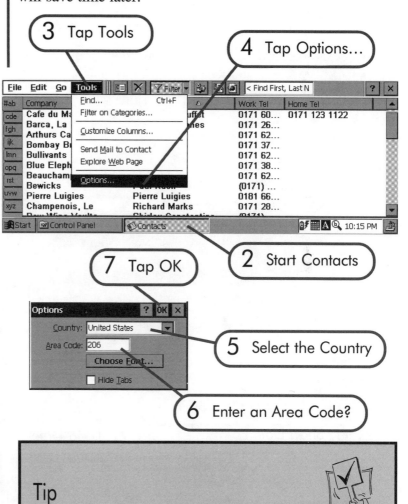

3 Tap Tools

4 Tap Options...

2 Start Contacts

7 Tap OK

5 Select the Country

6 Enter an Area Code?

Tip

If you will be entering a lot of contacts from different areas of your country or other countries then you may wish to leave these Options fields blank.

Tip

Keep an eye out for keyboard shortcuts. If there is one for a command, it is shown in the menu to the right of its name.

Communications dialing

If you are using your mobile device to dial up the Internet (see Chapter 7) you can set your area code and dialing prefixes in the Communications Properties panel.

You can enter details of any special places you call from regularly. In this example you will see how to enter your own dialing defaults and change the dialing patterns used. As standard Windows CE has 2 dialing locations: Home and Work.

To change the local area code, tap in the box, delete any existing contents using the delete or backspace keys and enter the new number. Enter your Country code in the same way.

1 Open the Control Panel.

2 Run Communications.

3 Tap the Dialing tab.

4 Select a dialing from location – Home or Work.

5 Set the local area and country codes.

6 Click Dialing Patterns.

7 Set the patterns as required and click OK.

8 Repeat steps 4 and 5 as necessary.

9 Tap OK.

3 Go to Dialing

4 Select a location

Communications Properties

| Device Name | Dialing | PC Connection |

When dialing from: **Work**   New...   Remove

Local settings are:

The local area code is: 206

The local country code is: 1

Dialing Patterns...

Dial using: ● Tone   ○ Pulse

☐ Disable call waiting by dialing:

Start | Control Panel | Contacts | Communications P... | 10:17 PM

9 Tap OK

6 Click Dialing Patterns

1 Open the Control Panel

5 Enter the codes

2 Double-tap Communications

Dialing Patterns   OK ×

You may determine the manner with which the phone is dialed by editing the Dialing Patterns for each type of call.

For Local calls dial:

9G

For Long Distance calls dial:

91FG

For International calls dial:

900EFG

(E,e = Country Code; F,f = Area Code; G,g = Number)

7 Set the patterns

Dialing patterns

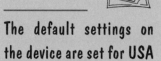

As the way that you dial numbers is different all over the world, these settings will need to be changed depending on where you are located. In the USA you dial 1 before the area code and number for a long distance, whereas in the UK you dial just the area code and number.

This is the section to enter any special dialing needs, e.g. if you have to enter a 9 for an outside line, or do not have to enter a 0 for a long distance call. The patterns are made up of the characters:

, (comma)	creates a pause of two seconds
E	the country code
F	the area code
G	the (local) phone number
0–9	digits to be dialed

For example, in my Work location, I have these patterns.

Local: 9G	9 for an outside line, but no pause, then the number
Long distance: 9FG	same as above but with the area code before the number
International: 900EFG	Specifies 9 for an outside line, 00 for international access, then the country code, area code and phone number.

With hotels around the world having different phone systems, getting a connection from a modem can be a challenge. You will probably have to experiment with pauses and possibly tone and pulse dialing (pulse dialing is much slower). For example:

Local: 9,,G	The two commas creates two pauses, each of 2 seconds

Data entry: Palm-size PC

The Palm-size PC has no physical keyboard – instead you enter information using a Software Input Panel. This has two faces: the first looks the same as a physical keyboard but is only displayed on screen; the second "Jot Character Recognizer" enables you to write directly on the screen with the stylus. Both these methods are referred to as entering data using the SIP – Software Input Panel. Choose whichever suits you best.

Jot Character Recognizer

The best way to learn to use the Jot is with the built-in Jot Tutorial. Work through it and learn how to form your characters so that the Jot can recognize them. The area of the screen shown in step 4 is where you enter text. In the tutorial, this screen shows you *where* you write letters / numbers and the special characters as well as *how* to write them.

❑ The Jot Tutorial

1 Tap the Keyboard Selector.

2 Select Jot Character Recognizer.

3 Tap Help.

4 Write the letters and numbers in the data entry area then click Next.

5 Select a category and a character and tap Show, or tap Show All for the whole set.

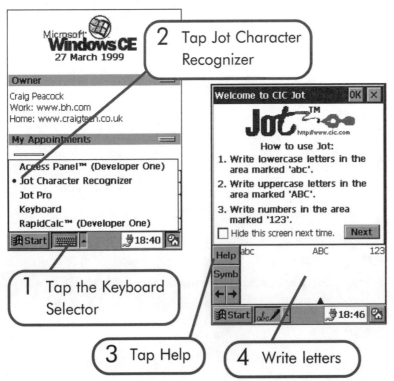

2 Tap Jot Character Recognizer

1 Tap the Keyboard Selector

3 Tap Help

4 Write letters

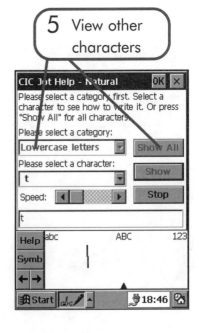

5 View other characters

20

The Software Input Panel: Keyboard

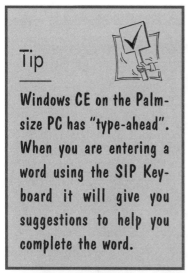
The SIP Keyboard should look very much like the keyboard on your PC, but with the small size of screen you can't see all the characters at once. Shown here are the lowercase and CAPS/Shift views. You can change the character sets by pressing the [áü] key to get accented letters, the [CAPS] and [áü] keys together, or the [Ctrl] key for further ranges of characters.

Normal – lower-case letters and numbers

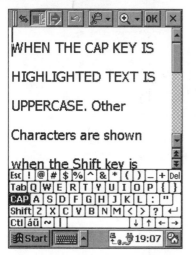

Use CAPS when you want to write in all capitals...

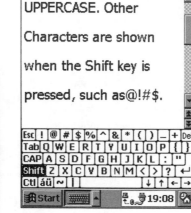

... or Shift for a single capital or other symbol

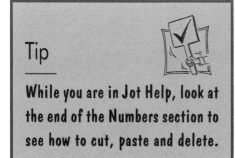

Password protecting

Having a password on your device is a good idea, in case it falls into the wrong hands. When a device is protected, the password must be entered every time the machine is switched on.

You can change your password at any time and as often as you feel is necessary.

Password protecting documents

On the Handheld PC it is possible to password protect documents and spreadsheets, This is useful if you have confidential documents that you want to keep safe.

❑ Handheld PC

1 Open the Control Panel.

2 Run Password.

3 Enter your password – and again to confirm.

4 Tap OK.

❑ Protecting documents from within Pocket Word or Excel

5 Tap File and select Password.

6 At the dialog box enter the password twice and tap OK.

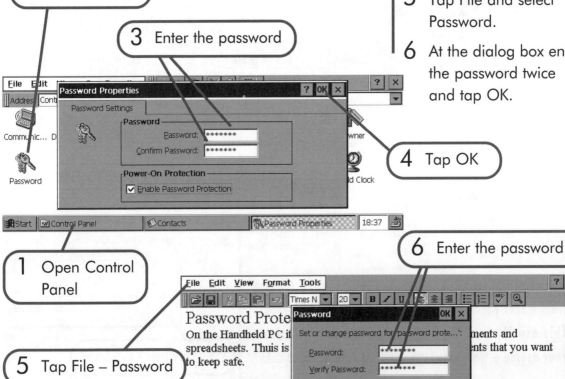

2 Run Password

3 Enter the password

4 Tap OK

1 Open Control Panel

5 Tap File – Password

6 Enter the password

TAKE NOTE - If you forget your password their is no way of getting back into it, so be very careful with password protected documents.

Basic steps Palm-size PC

- ❏ Palm-size PC

1 Tap Start, then Settings and select Password.

2 Tap the Keyboard Selector and select the keyboard.

3 Tap into the Password box and enter your password, then enter it again in the Confirm password box.

4 Tap OK.

- ❏ Starting up

5 Display the keyboard.

6 Enter your password.

When switching on your Palm-size PC device, you will be presented with a password dialog box, but as there is no physical keyboard, you will need to bring up the Software Input Panel to enter your password.

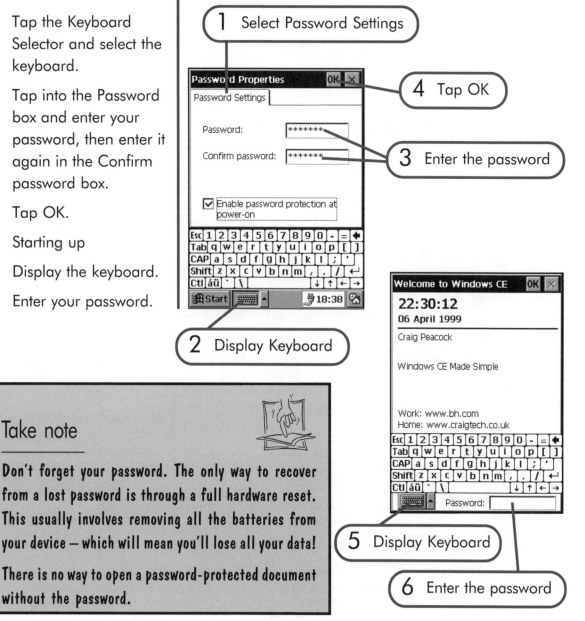

1 Select Password Settings

4 Tap OK

3 Enter the password

2 Display Keyboard

5 Display Keyboard

6 Enter the password

Take note

Don't forget your password. The only way to recover from a lost password is through a full hardware reset. This usually involves removing all the batteries from your device – which will mean you'll lose all your data!

There is no way to open a password-protected document without the password.

Sounds and alarms

All Windows CE devices are capable of playing sounds from files in the WAV format, which can be transferred from a PC or recorded directly on those machines with a voice recorder.

The sounds can be linked to alarms, or notifications of appointments (see page 33) and to "events." These are actions such as when a window is maximized or minimized, when you send someone a contact via Infrared or when a task is due.

Using your own favorite sounds

A lot of people have their favorite sounds for various events or alarms. A friend of mine has his son's voice for when it's time to wake up and his wife's for when he is meeting friends and family.

The standard sounds are in the \Windows folder. Your own WAV files can be saved in any folder on the device. You can browse for them using the Browse button in the Event Sound section.

When you record your own sounds in the Voice Recorder application they are saved in the \My Documents folder unless you specify elsewhere. See Chapter 9 for more details on the Voice recorder.

1 Open the Control Panel and tap Volume & Sounds.

2 On the Volume tab tick the actions for which you want sounds.

3 Set the levels for Clicks & Taps.

4 Tap the Sound tab.

5 Tap the Event Name to which you wish to assign a sound.

6 Tap the Event Sound drop-down box and select a sound.

or

7 Tap Browse and locate the file to use your own sound.

8 Tap the Play button to preview the sound.

❑ Repeat steps 6 to 9 for every event you wish to link to a sound.

9 Tap OK.

Tip

To make your sounds louder, move the volume slider towards the top. I have mine set one from the bottom and I think that is quite loud enough.

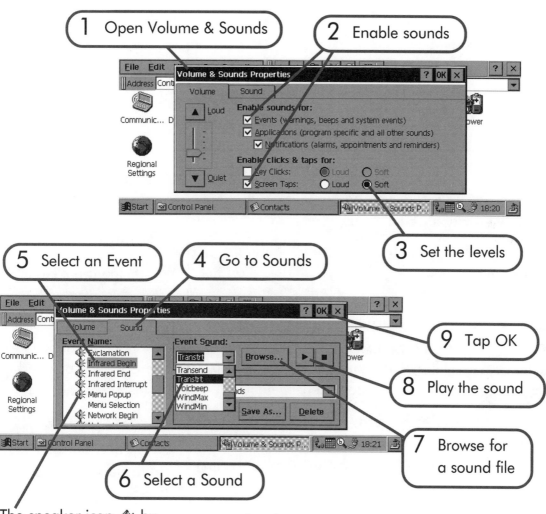

1 Open Volume & Sounds

2 Enable sounds

3 Set the levels

5 Select an Event

4 Go to Sounds

9 Tap OK

8 Play the sound

7 Browse for a sound file

6 Select a Sound

The speaker icon 📢 by an event description means there is a sound associated with it.

Sound schemes

When you have finished associating sounds with events, you can save the settings as a sound scheme – you might want to have a quiet scheme for use in the office and a noisier, but cheerier one to use at home. Just tap the Save As button and give the scheme an appropriate name.

To change between sound schemes, tap the drop-down box in the scheme section and select the appropriate scheme.

Summary

❏ You can customize your Windows CE device to suit the country you live in.

❏ If most of your contacts live in the same country or area, set the default phone codes in Contacts.

❏ You can change how your Windows CE device dials phone numbers. This is useful for when you have to dial a 9 or other prefix during dial-up networking.

❏ The handwriting recognition program Jot is included on every Windows CE Palm-size device.

❏ To access different character sets on the Software Input Panel Keyboard tap the CAP, Shift, Ctrl or áü key.

❏ Setting a password on your device will help keep your data safe should your device fall into the wrong hands, but don't forget the password as there is no way of opening a protected document without it.

❏ Customizing your device with selected sounds can make your machine a little more personal. You can use a favorite sound for Calendar alarms.

3 Pocket Outlook

Calendar

This section covers the main features of three applications in the Pocket Outlook suite – Calendar, Contacts and Tasks. With these, you can create, delete and move appointments as well as inviting other people to meetings and attach notes to those appointments. Using calendar in conjunction with the World Clock (see Chapter 9) allows you to create meetings – at the right times! – around the world.

Later, in Chapter 6, you will meet ActiveSync, which automates the job of copying data between your PC and mobile device. This negates the need to retype information and means changes on either machine can be easily transferred to the other – simply connect the two together and it's done. The Calendar is one of the most important applications to synchronize in this way.

Here are all the options and icons on the Calendar screen (from an H/PC Professional).

Calendar symbols

Some or all of these may be displayed to the left of the appointment

🔔 Alarm set

📝 Note present

🐢 Meeting arranged

🏠 Location set

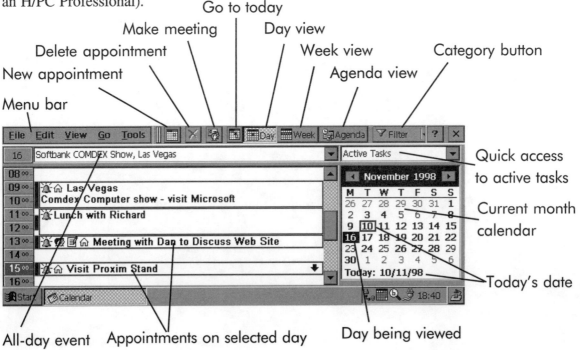

Go to today

Make meeting   Day view

Delete appointment   Week view   Category button

New appointment   Agenda view

Menu bar

Quick access to active tasks

Current month calendar

Today's date

All-day event   Appointments on selected day   Day being viewed

Basic steps

1 Tap the Week view.

2 Tap View.

❑ Number of days

3 Tap Number of days.

4 Select the number you would like to see.

❑ Time slots

5 Tap View.

6 Tap Half-hour slots.

Calendar Views

When you first launch Calendar you are presented with a view showing the current day. To navigate around your system you have several different options. You can jump to a particular date, scroll through month by month, change the views to see the next week (on the H/PC Pro you even have month and year views).

The Week view

To accommodate different working weeks, the calendar application can be easily customized to view a different number of days. Here's how to modify the week view.

Experiment with different numbers of days showing to find out which method you like best. In the example below you can see a five-day work week with half-hour slots.

Display previous/
next week

Half-hour slots

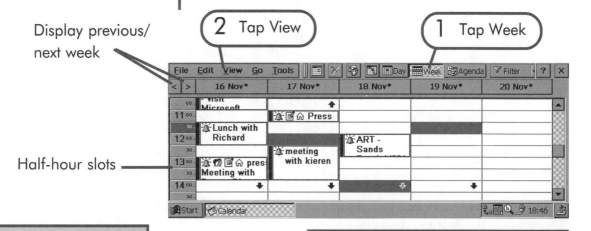

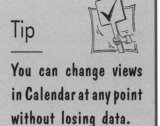

Tip

You can change views in Calendar at any point without losing data.

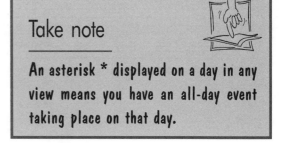

Take note

An asterisk * displayed on a day in any view means you have an all-day event taking place on that day.

Calendar on the H/PC Pro

The Handheld PC Professional has several extra features in the calendar application that are not included as standard on the Handheld PC. These include month and year views.

In the Month view:

- The * refers to an all-day event

- Colored areas show the times when you have meetings. In the screen shot you can see that on the 9th of October for example, I have meetings from 9am to 12 noon, and 3pm to 6pm. These are represented with two 12-hour clocks.

- The year view shows days where you have an appointment or all-day event as bold.

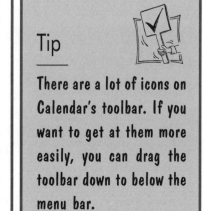

Tip

There are a lot of icons on Calendar's toolbar. If you want to get at them more easily, you can drag the toolbar down to below the menu bar.

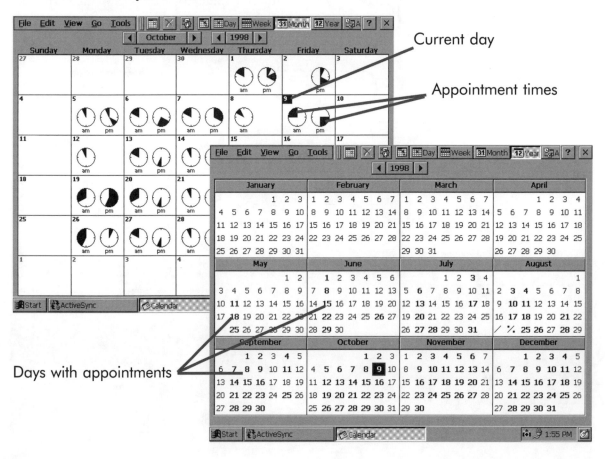

Days with appointments

Current day

Appointment times

Basic steps

1 Tap the Go menu.

2 Tap Go to Date.

3 Type in the date or use the right arrow key or the pen to select it.

4 If you press the drop-down box, it will bring up the date-picker dialog box, showing the selected date.

5 To go to the selected date tap OK.

Jumping to a date

The **Go** menu has various options for navigating around Outlook and moving through the Calendar – the one to use for this is **Go to Date**.

Take note

On the PC Pro, you can jump to any day of the year, by tapping the day in the Year view.

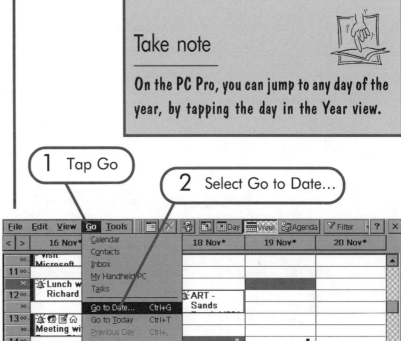

1 Tap Go

2 Select Go to Date...

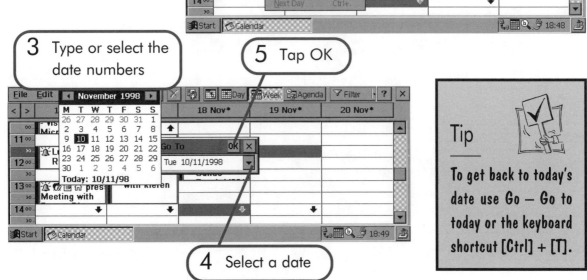

3 Type or select the date numbers

5 Tap OK

4 Select a date

Tip

To get back to today's date use Go — Go to today or the keyboard shortcut [Ctrl] + [T].

Calendar entries

There are three ways to make a new appointment – decide which works best for you.

There are three icons above the note box (see the screenshot below).

Notes – You can make notes about this appointment by tapping the "Tap here to add notes box."

Category – Put this appointment in a particular category then select it from there.

Contacts – Invite others to the meeting via e-mail (see page 40).

1 Tap the New Appointment button.

or

2 Tap File, then tap New Appointment.

or

3 Press [Ctrl] + [N].

4 Enter the description.

5 Enter a location or select a previous location from the drop-down box.

6 Enter the Starts and Ends date and time.

7 If this item is to occur regularly tap the drop-down box. If your occurrence pattern is not listed tap the <Edit pattern ....> line to add a new one.

8 Check the All day event box if needed.

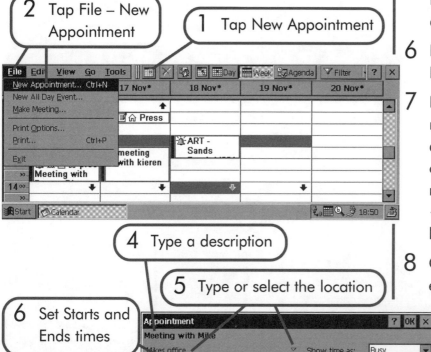

2 Tap File – New Appointment

1 Tap New Appointment

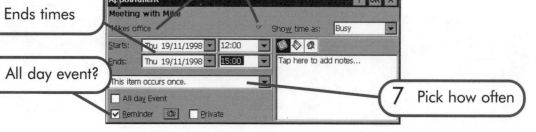

4 Type a description

5 Type or select the location

6 Set Starts and Ends times

8 All day event?

7 Pick how often

Appointment categories

❏ **To create a category**

1 Tap .

2 Tap the Edit Category List... button.

3 Enter the name of the new category.

4 Tap Add.

5 Tap OK.

❏ **Filtering**

6 Tap ▽ Filter ▼ the Filter button.

7 Select a filter, e.g. Work. Now you'll see the other unfiltered appointments disappear from view!

❏ **Displaying all your appointments**

8 Tap the filter button.

9 Select all items.

When you create appointments, it's possible for you to assign a category to that meeting.

The Category button has been changed between Windows CE 2.0 on the Handheld PC and the H/PC Professional. On Windows CE 2.0 it is labeled as Filter, in the latest version of Windows CE it shows you the category you have filtered upon. Don't worry, as it functions the same in both versions.

Filters and categories are the easiest methods of breaking down a large list of contacts or appointments and they are incredibly handy if you work on lots of projects, as you can use them to see only the appointments in a given category.

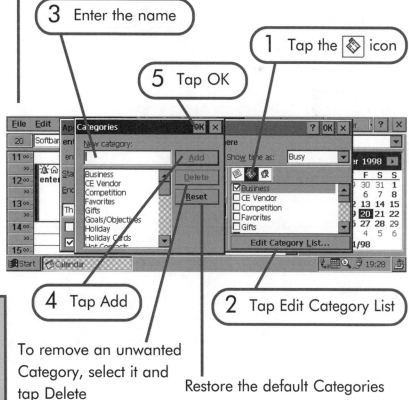

3 Enter the name

5 Tap OK

1 Tap the ◈ icon

4 Tap Add

2 Tap Edit Category List

Take note

You can assign an entry to more than one category.

To remove an unwanted Category, select it and tap Delete

Restore the default Categories

Notes, Categories and Contacts

You can add some Notes to this meeting, to remind you of any important facts, or use Categories to help organize your data, or the Contacts to invite others to a meeting. In my example I've typed directions on how to find a contact's office and drawn a map to help.

1 Tap the "Tap here to add notes… " box.

2 The Inkwriter window will open. Type in a note or draw a sketch on the screen.

❑ To set a Category

3 Tap ◈ then tap the box to the left of the required Category.

❑ To add a Contact

4 Tap ⚑ then tap on the Contacts list and select a name.

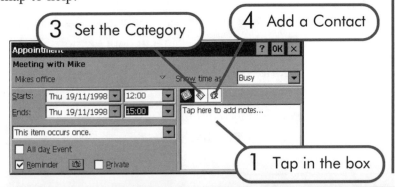

3 Set the Category

4 Add a Contact

1 Tap in the box

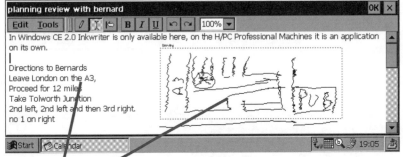

2 Type a note or draw a sketch

When back on the main screen this appointment now has four visual indicators on it.

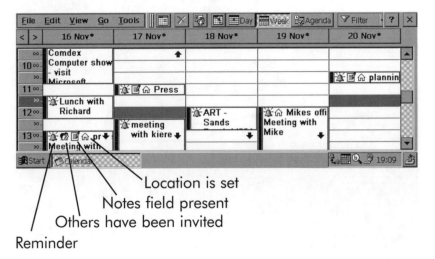

Location is set

Notes field present

Others have been invited

Reminder

Basic steps

1 Set up an appoint-
ment.

2 Tick the Reminder
check box.

3 Tap the bell icon.

4 Set the reminder time
as required.

5 Tap Reminders Op-
tions…

6 Select a sound from
the drop-down list.

7 Tap to clear the ticks
from the Interrupt me
with a message and
Flashing light boxes if
not required.

8 Tap OK.

9 Tap OK again at the
Reminder Defaults
dialog box.

Tip

Use the message or light
instead of the sound if you
don't want to disturb
nearby colleagues.

Setting the Alarm

If you want advance notification of an appointment you can turn
on the Reminder and set its timing and method.

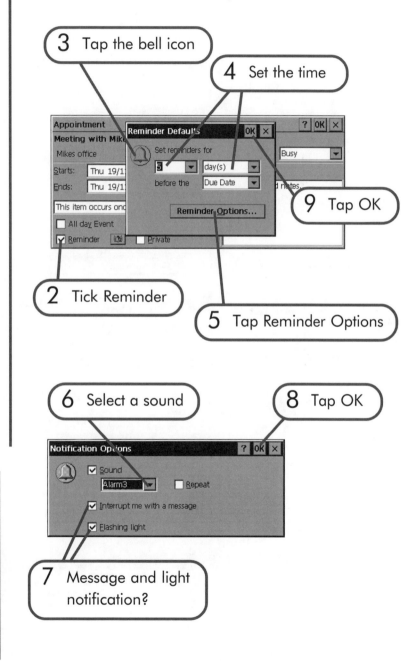

3 Tap the bell icon

4 Set the time

9 Tap OK

2 Tick Reminder

5 Tap Reminder Options

6 Select a sound

8 Tap OK

7 Message and light
notification?

All day events

When you want to add an all day event it is relatively easy – you simply check the all day event box when creating an appointment. Deleting one, on the other hand, is a little trickier.

When you've created an all day event, its description will appear just under the icon bar. To see any other all day events for the current day tap the drop-down box.

Deleting an all day event

When you want to delete an all day event, you will have to be in the Agenda view. It is the only screen within Calendar that allows you to delete the event.

Basic steps

1 Select the day and double-tap a blank time to create an appointment.

2 Enter a description.

3 Tap the All day event check box.

4 Tap OK.

❑ Deleting an event

5 Tap the Agenda icon.

6 All day events are at the top of the Appointments and Events list. Tap the event to highlight it.

7 Tap ☒ the Delete icon or press [Ctrl]+[D].

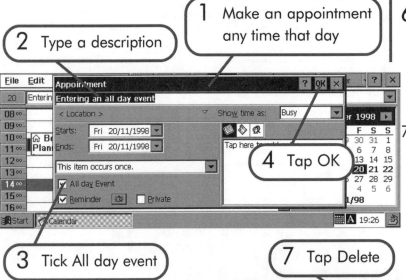

1 Make an appointment any time that day

2 Type a description

4 Tap OK

3 Tick All day event

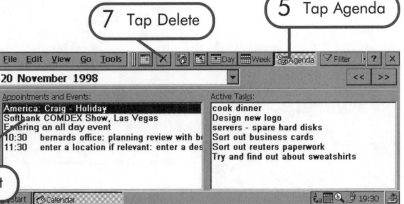

7 Tap Delete

5 Tap Agenda

6 Select the event

36

Basic steps

Adjusting meeting times

❏ Changing duration

1 Tap View then tap Half-hour slots.

2 Tap the appointment.

3 You will see arrows (or drag bars) at the top and bottom of the appointment. Tap and drag a bar slowly up or down. Lift the pen to set the new time.

❏ Moving times

4 Tap the appointment to get the drag bars.

5 Press in the middle of the appointment and drag to another day or another time on the same day.

The appointment times are displayed

Meeting times are sometimes changed. Here are a couple of different ways of changing/moving appointments.

When you tap an appointment, drag bars appear. These allow you to alter an appointment without having to type in new times.

Changing the duration

You can change the start and/or end time of a meeting. In the example, I'm working in Day view, but this can be done in Week view just as easily.

Moving appointment times

To move an appointment between days or to a different time on the same day, tap with the stylus and drag.

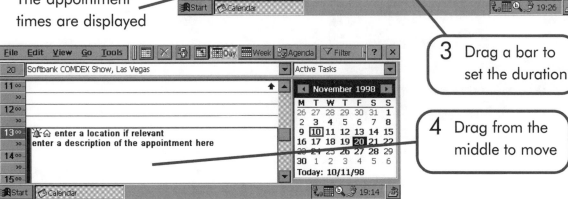

1 Tap View – Half-hour slots

2 Tap the appointment

3 Drag a bar to set the duration

4 Drag from the middle to move

Moving appointments between weeks/months

You can't drag meetings to different weeks or months. If you want to do this, you must use the same dialog box that was used when you created the appointment.

Basic steps

1 Go to either Day or Week view.

2 Double-tap on the appointment.

3 Change the Starts or Ends date and/or time settings as required.

4 Tap OK. Your appointment will have been moved.

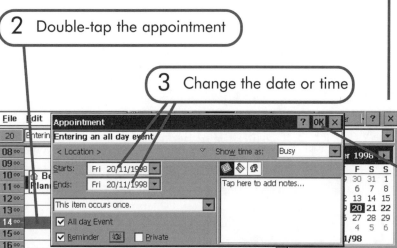

2 Double-tap the appointment

3 Change the date or time

4 Tap OK

Tip

Any other features of the appointment can also be changed. Just double-tap the appointment to reopen this dialog box and click OK when you are done.

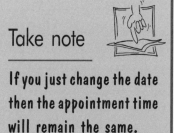

Take note

If you just change the date then the appointment time will remain the same.

Basic steps

1 Tap the Tools menu and select Find.

or

2 Drag the toolbar to the left to display all the icons and tap the Find icon 📇.

3 In the Find box, type the name or text to search for.

4 Change the Type of search if you know in which area the item will be.

5 Tap Find Now.

6 When the search results window is displayed, double-tap on the description to be taken to the screen for that appointment, where you can read or edit it as required.

7 Tap ✕ in the top right corner to close the Find window.

Quite often you need to search for contacts, appointments or even details of where a meeting is to take place. One of the icons you first revealed when you moved the calendar bar is the Find icon. It is normally hidden away on the far right-hand side of the menu bar and it allows you to search for text in a variety of the Microsoft Outlook packages including e-mail, contacts, tasks and appointments.

For best results, use a name or location or a significant word that should be in the desired item – and in few others.

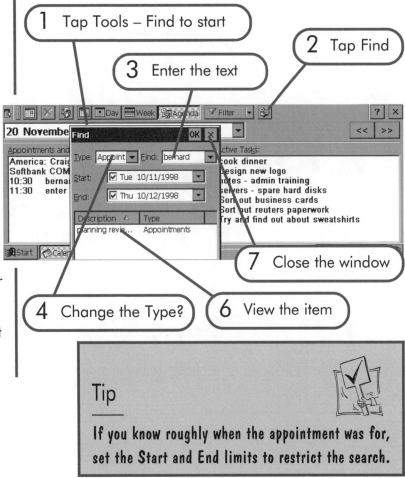

1 Tap Tools – Find to start

2 Tap Find

3 Enter the text

4 Change the Type?

6 View the item

7 Close the window

Tip

If you know roughly when the appointment was for, set the Start and End limits to restrict the search.

Contacts

The Contacts application is where you keep your names, addresses and other contact details. It is a powerful application with lots of views, plus the ability to sort your contacts. You can customize the columns to meet your needs. Over the next few pages you'll see how to use these features.

The integration with the other Windows CE applications is one of the major features of the Contacts application. From the main view you can e-mail, make a meeting or visit a Web site for a particular contact.

Take note

When you enter or modify a contact on your Handheld PC, the next time you synchronize with your desktop PC the updates will show up there.

New contact

Create appointment/meeting request

Delete contact

Create message / E-mail

Menu bar

Filter contacts

Quick Search bar

Help

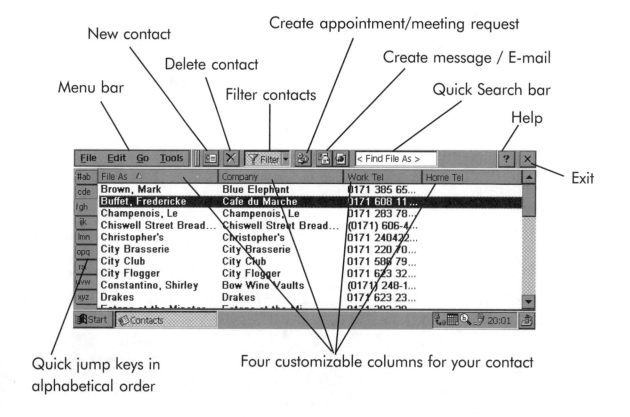

Exit

	File As △	Company	Work Tel	Home Tel
#ab				
cde	Brown, Mark	Blue Elephant	0171 385 65...	
fgh	Buffet, Fredericke	Cafe du Marche	0171 608 11...	
ijk	Champenois, Le	Champenois, Le	0171 283 78...	
lmn	Chiswell Street Bread...	Chiswell Street Bread...	(0171) 606-4...	
opq	Christopher's	Christopher's	0171 240422...	
rs	City Brasserie	City Brasserie	0171 220 70...	
uvw	City Club	City Club	0171 588 79...	
xyz	City Flogger	City Flogger	0171 623 32...	
	Constantino, Shirley	Bow Wine Vaults	(0171) 248-1...	
	Drakes	Drakes	0171 623 23...	

Start Contacts   20:01

Quick jump keys in alphabetical order

Four customizable columns for your contact

Basic steps

1 Tap the New Contact icon.

2 Enter the Name and other details on the Business panel.

3 Click 🏠 to open the Personal panel to add details there.

4 Click 🖼 to add a Note or a Category.

5 Tap the Notetaker area to type a note using Inkwriter.

6 Tick one or more Categories as needed.

7 Tap OK to save the data and exit.

Creating a Contact

When creating a contact on Windows CE devices you have lots of options and three main screens. It's possible to categorize your contacts, add notes and keep details on all your regular contact fields such as e-mail, work / home fax numbers, Web site address, etc.

Here are the three screens when creating a new contact.

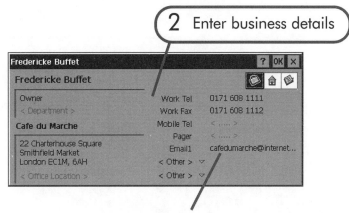

2 Enter business details

You can store more than one e-mail address per contact

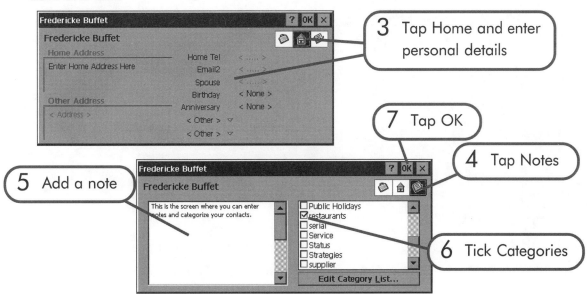

3 Tap Home and enter personal details

7 Tap OK

4 Tap Notes

5 Add a note

6 Tick Categories

Views in Contacts

Earlier you localized the Contacts application by telling it which country you live in. You can now see how to modify the columns to get the view you want.

There are over 50 possible options to choose from and that, and the fact that only a few can actually be viewed without scrolling at any one time, means you need to think about what information you would like to see at a glance.

Basic steps

1 Tap Tools then tap Customize Columns.

❏ To remove a field

2 Select the field and tap Remove field.

❏ To add a field

3 Select it from the list and tap Add field.

❏ Change the order

4 Tap the field in the right-hand pane and tap Move Up or Move Down to reposition it.

5 Tap OK.

6 If you have a lot of contacts, a warning will appear about the time it will take to complete this task. Tap OK to continue and the columns will change.

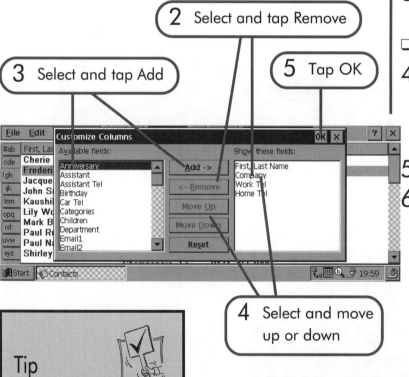

2 Select and tap Remove

3 Select and tap Add

5 Tap OK

4 Select and move up or down

Tip

If you have more than four columns, a horizontal scroll bar will be added to the Contacts display.

Take note

The order of the list top to bottom is displayed left to right on the screen.

Basic steps

❏ To sort on a column

1 Tap the title bar of a column to sort on its contents. The contents of the Quick Search field change to match the sort column.

❏ To change the order

2 Tap the title bar again to switch between ascending and descending sort order.

❏ Searching

3 Tap the title bar of the desired column.

4 Tap the Quick Search field.

5 Enter the first letter of name you want. The people that begin with that letter appear.

Or

6 Tap Tools then Find (or press [Ctrl] + [F]) and use the Find box as shown on page 39.

The arrowhead icon in a column tells you that this is the column you are currently sorting your contacts on. It is also the column on which you can quick search for your contacts.

Searching

The quickest way to find a contact is to use the quick search bar but, as in the Calendar section, there is a Find option. An alternate method is to use bFIND if you have it (see page 139).

1 Tap the title bar

2 Tap to reverse the sort

3 Tap the title bar

4 Tap Quick Search

5 Enter the first letter

Tasks

The Tasks application that comes with Windows CE includes all the features you've seen in the previous sections. Good integration with the Calendar and the other Microsoft Windows CE applications is another strength of this application.

In the next few pages I'll take you through the different options in the Tasks application. I will show you how to create, delete and organize tasks. The application functions identically on different versions of Windows CE though its appearance (the Quick Edit panel) has changed.

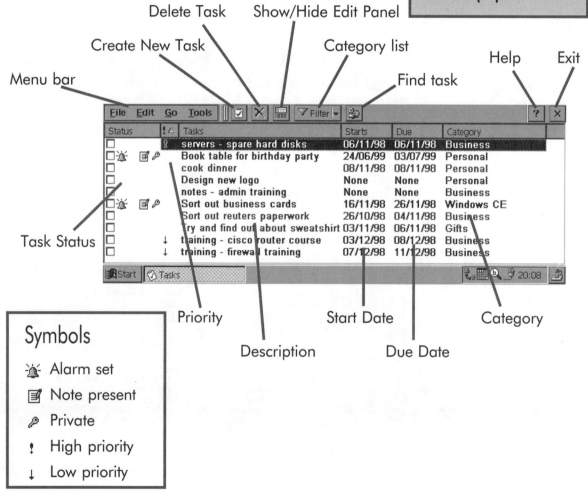

Take note

On certain versions of Windows CE you have to select the type of filter and then the category, otherwise you'll get all tasks displayed.

Delete Task

Create New Task

Show/Hide Edit Panel

Category list

Menu bar

Find task

Help

Exit

Task Status

Symbols

☼ Alarm set

📝 Note present

🔑 Private

! High priority

↓ Low priority

Priority

Description

Start Date

Due Date

Category

Basic steps

Creating a new Task

1 Tap 🖩 the Show Edit panel icon to reveal the new task display.

2 Enter a Description.

3 Select a Priority from the drop-down list.

4 Select the Start and Due dates.

5 If the date is in the far future, tap the drop-down box in the start field, then tap on the name to select a month.

   If the task is due next year, tap the year. A small box will open – type in the year or scroll to the number.

6 To categorize the task, tap the Category... button and select one from the list (or create a new one if needed).

7 Tap Enter.

You can enter a task really quickly through the Quick Edit panel on a Windows CE 2.0 device. In this example I'll show you how to create a new task and use the date picker to select a future date.

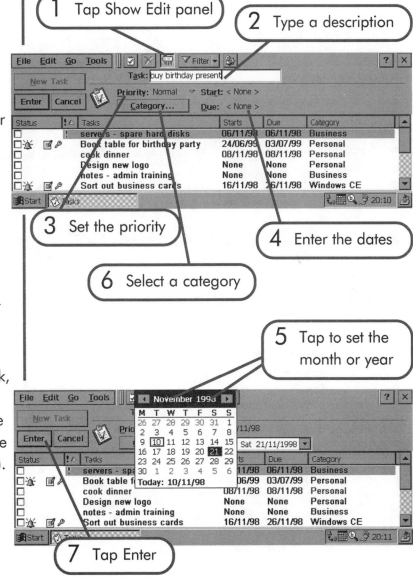

1 Tap Show Edit panel

2 Type a description

3 Set the priority

4 Enter the dates

6 Select a category

5 Tap to set the month or year

7 Tap Enter

45

Creating a new Task in the dialog box

While the core details are the same as before, the full dialog box method also allows you to type some notes regarding the Task, create repeat Tasks (e.g., weekly reminders for reports, etc.) and associate alarms with the task.

follow the steps on page 33.

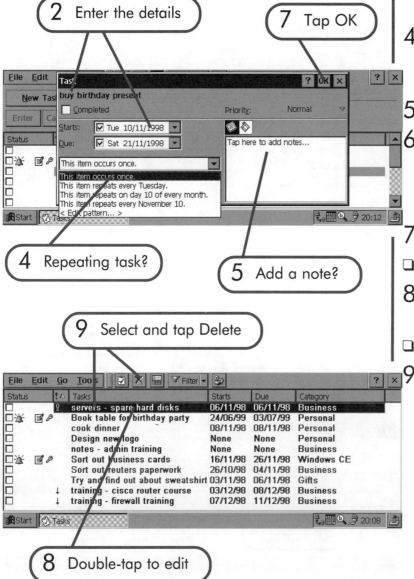

2 — Enter the details

7 — Tap OK

4 — Repeating task?

5 — Add a note?

9 — Select and tap Delete

8 — Double-tap to edit

Basic steps

1   Tap ☑ the New Task icon.

2   Enter a Description and set the Priority and dates as on the quick Edit panel.

4   If the Task must be repeated, pick an occurrence pattern.

5   Add a note if wanted.

6   If you want to set a reminder alarm, follow the steps on page 33.

7   Tap OK.

❑   To edit a Task

8   Double-tap it to open the task dialog box.

❑   To delete a Task

9   Tap the Task to select it, then tap ☒ the Delete icon or tap Edit – Delete Task.

Basic steps

1 Tap the type of filter – All, Active or Completed Tasks.

2 Tap the Category. You will then see those Tasks that fit the selected criteria.

3 To return to showing all the Tasks, deselect any categories by tapping on Filter then selecting All Tasks.

4 On H/PC Pro and Palm-size PCs you also have to deselect the category.

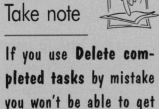

Take note

If you use Delete completed tasks by mistake you won't be able to get your completed tasks back!

Categories within Tasks

The Tasks option not only allows you to display categories but also to show only active or completed Tasks within a category.

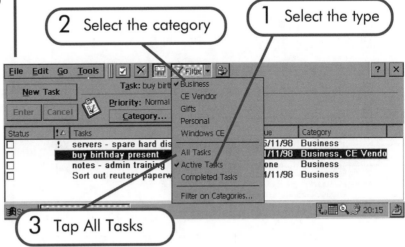

When Tasks are completed

When you have finished a Task you can check it off by putting a check in the status box to the left of its description. When you want to delete your completed Tasks, tap the **Edit** menu and select **Delete completed tasks**. You will be asked to confirm the deletions.

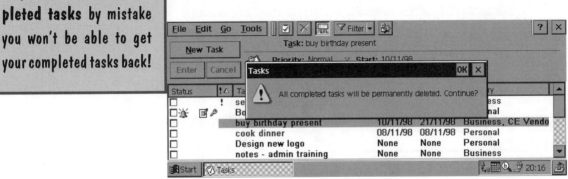

Summary

- [ ] The Calendar application has lots of different views to help you browse your appointments, you can even change the number of working days you'd like displayed.

- [ ] Jumping to a particular date can save you time compared to scrolling through days/weeks.

- [ ] Moving and changing appointment times can be done with a quick drag of the stylus.

- [ ] Creating categories for your meetings/tasks can help if you have a busy schedule, especially if you want to be able to quickly view a subset of all your stored information.

- [ ] The Find routine offers an easy way to track down appointments, contacts and other information within Outlook.

- [ ] The Contacts application will hold the details of your contacts efficiently.

- [ ] Changing the views within Contacts can make finding key information quicker and easier.

- [ ] Tasks are created and stored in much the same way as appointments.

4 Documents and notes

What is a folder?

Basic steps

1 Tap My Handheld PC.

2 If you want to create the folder within another one, open the existing folder now.

3 Tap File and select New Folder.

4 Tap the folder name and change it so that it identifies what will be stored in it.

Folder, still sometimes called directories, can contain files and other folders. Folders are a good way to organize your files and documents, allowing you to store files, notes, voice recorded memos in individual areas, so that they can be located easily when you next need them.

Until you create new folders, all your documents will be saved in the \My Documents folder and as it fills up it will become increasingly difficult to find things. Creating new folders is the easy solution.

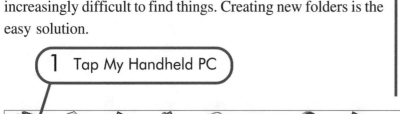

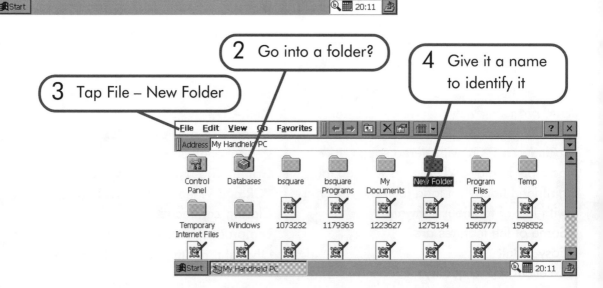

50

Basic steps

Pocket Word

❏ Starting Pocket Word

1 Double-tap the Pocket Word icon from the main screen. This will automatically open up a new document.

2 Type in some text so that you can explore some of the features of Pocket Word.

3 Save the document – tap the 🖫 icon.

At the Save dialog box, type in a suitable filename.

4 Tap OK.

This is a cutdown version of the desktop version of Microsoft Word, but still packed with features such as document templates, outline views, multiple fonts, various font sizes, **bold,** *italics*, search and replace, bulleted and numbered lists, spell checker and the ability to password-protect documents.

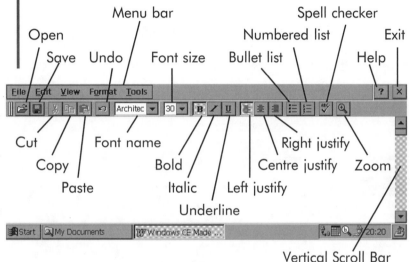

Sample text

Try this sample text – complete with errors!

Product Review
The product reviewed was a in car audio and TV entertainment system for my car, it included a 9" TV with stereo sound. It was possible to play DVD Movies to keep the girlfriend happy on long journeys. It came with lots of fabulous software.
Some of the features are
Easy install
Excellent sound qualiry

Easy removal for security
Multi-CD Autochanger
Support for multiple displays
Headphone support
Games and multimedia suport
VCR and Video camera support.
Closing comments
The product is excellent it works better than I thought. not that good value for money.

Editing and formatting

You can tap anywhere on the screen to move the cursor to that location or you can use the arrow keys. There are also lots of keyboard shortcuts for navigating around Pocket Word. To see these, tap the Help button and scroll down to Shortcuts.

Text can be formatted with the buttons or by selecting options from the Format menu.

● Either select the text and apply the formats;

● or set the formats before typing new text.

This document would look better with the title in bold, centered and in a larger font. The features can appear in a bulletted list and "Closing comments" can be in bold.

1 To select text, tap to its left, then gently drag the stylus across the text, highlighting it.

2 Tap the formats button(s) as required.

3 Tap anywhere on the document to deselect the text.

❑ Lists

4 Select the list.

5 Tap the ▤ Bulleted or ▤ Numbered List button, or tap Format – Paragraph and Style and select from there.

6 To add more, tap at the end of the last line and press [Enter]. Bullets (or numbers) are put in for you.

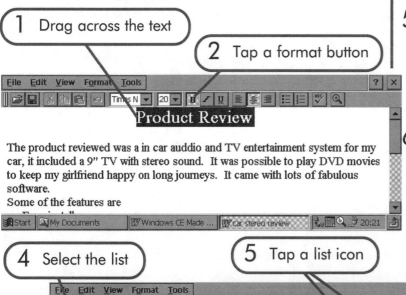

1 Drag across the text

2 Tap a format button

4 Select the list

5 Tap a list icon

Basic steps

❏ Zooming in

1 Tap the Zoom button
🔍.

2 Tap the zoom icon
again to go to the next
zoom level.

❏ Setting the zoom level

3 Tap View, then Zoom.

4 Select a percentage
from the list.

or

5 Tap Custom... and
enter a number.

Tip

Experiment with the zoom feature, it can be very useful.

Take note

If you have two or more Microsoft Pocket Word or Excel documents open, press [Ctrl] and [.] or press [Ctrl] and [,] to move between them.

The Zoom feature

To be able to see more of the text we've just altered on the screen you can use the zoom feature, with its multiple levels.

When you are entering text, zoom in close enough to be able to read it comfortably. When you are formatting it, and need to see how the overall layout will look, zoom back out far enough to get the full (printed) page width across the screen.

The defaults are good but you can manually specify zoom levels between 50% and up to 200% of the text size. Tap View, Zoom, Custom....

The screenshot below shows Word at the 50% zoom level.

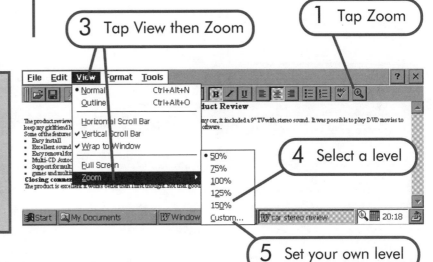

3 Tap View then Zoom

1 Tap Zoom

4 Select a level

5 Set your own level

Spell checking

Before you finish your document you may want to spell check it. Like most of the options on Windows CE there is more than one way to bring up the spell checker.

When the spell checker meets a word it does not recognize, it will prompt you with suggested corrections (if it can). The word is not necessarily wrong – it's just not in Word's dictionary.

You can then:

● accept a suggestion;

● retype the word if you can see your mistake;

● ignore it – and all future occurrences – if it is correct;

● add it to the dictionary.

1 Tap the Spell check button .

or

2 Tap to open the Tools menu, then tap Spelling.

or

3 Press [Ctrl] + [7].

4 If the word is correct, tap Ignore, Ignore All or Add, to add it to the dictionary.

5 If the first suggestion is correct, press [Enter].

Otherwise

6 Tap the down arrow and select from the list of alternative words.

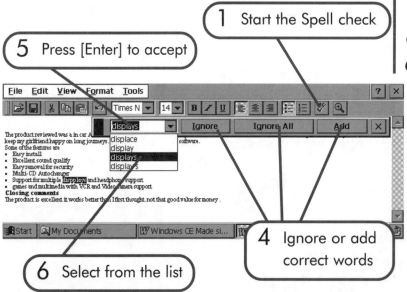

1 Start the Spell check

5 Press [Enter] to accept

6 Select from the list

4 Ignore or add correct words

Copying and pasting text

1 Highlight a section of text – tap and drag over the text you want to select.

2 Tap 🖹 the Copy button.

or

3 Tap Edit – Copy.

4 Move to where the text is to go, or open a new document.

5 Tap 🖹 the Paste button.

or

6 Tap Edit – Paste.

Copying and Pasting can save you a lot of repetitive typing and it's very handy when you want to create a template from an existing document.

Text can be copied and pasted in nearly all Microsoft Windows CE applications or it can be copied and pasted in the same document.

Try copying and pasting some text from your new document.

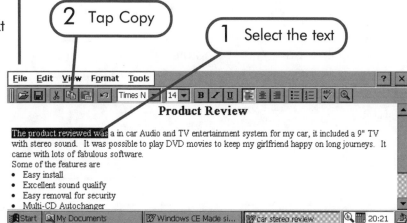

2 Tap Copy

1 Select the text

5 Tap Paste

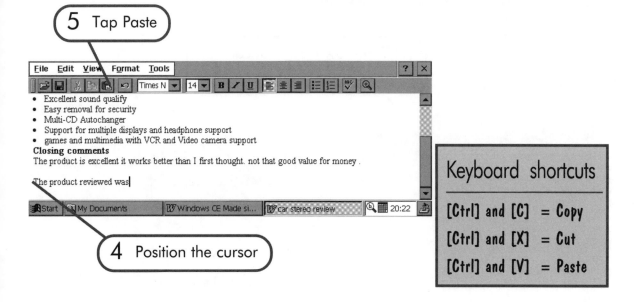

4 Position the cursor

Keyboard shortcuts

[Ctrl] and [C] = Copy

[Ctrl] and [X] = Cut

[Ctrl] and [V] = Paste

Pocket Word templates

One of the methods of saving time when creating documents on Windows CE is to create a template – a document which has the formats in place and basic data already filled in. Some examples of uses of templates are minutes of meetings, short reports, overview documents and reminder lists.

The previous document could form the basis of a template. First delete any surplus text, leaving the heading and any other text that will be wanted in similar reviews, plus the start of the body text, bullet list and samples of any other formatted paragraphs.

❑ Saving templates

1 Tap File then Save As and Shortcut to Office Templates.

2 Tap the Type drop-down box and select Pocket Word Template.

3 Give it a meaningful name.

4 Tap OK.

❑ Using templates

5 Tap File, then New then Document from Template.

6 Select a template and click OK.

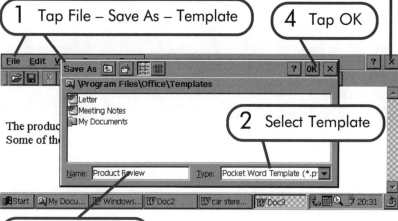

1 Tap File – Save As – Template

4 Tap OK

2 Select Template

3 Give it a name

5 Tap File – New – Document from Template

6 Select a template

Take note

When giving the template a name, note that documents created from it will have that as the first part of their names.

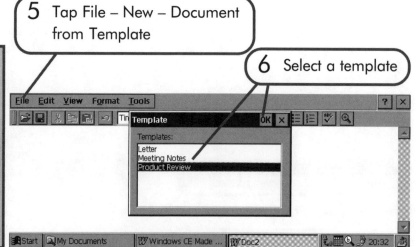

Notetaker

Tip

To find out the hardware and keyboard shortcuts in Notetaker, tap Start – Help, and then select Notetaker Shortcuts. You will only use a few in our examples, but try them out – they can really save a lot of time.

The Palm-size PC Notetaker is designed to take notes quickly and easily. Its many features include handwriting and text input, templates, different text styles, multiple fonts and font sizes, and even drawing on the screen.

First, I'll give you an overview of the application, highlighting what the icons mean.

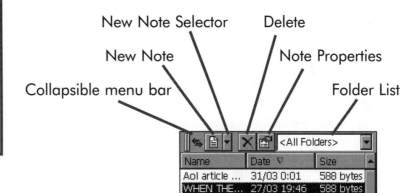

File menu commands

New   All your note templates are shown here

Open   Opens a filed note

Save As   Notes can be saved so they are viewable in other applications (such as Microsoft Word on the PC)

Delete   Deletes selected note(s)

Rename   Renames a selected note

Folders   All your folders for organizing your notes

Properties   Rename and move notes to different folders

Send-To   Send a note via e-mail or Infra-Red

Receive   Receive a note via Infra-Red

Creating a note

In the File New Note menu, you can create a note based on an existing template, or you can create your own templates.

When you are writing a note, another set of buttons is displayed at the top of the screen. These enable you to edit, format and zoom in on your text.

Basic steps

1 Tap the collapsible menu bar and select File – New – Meeting Notes.

or

2 Tap the New Note Selector button and select Meeting Notes.

3 Tap the Software Input Panel to open it. The Text tool is automatically selected.

4 Tap to the right of the Subject: and enter any text on that line.

5 Continue down the screen, adding text as required to the right of the other headings.

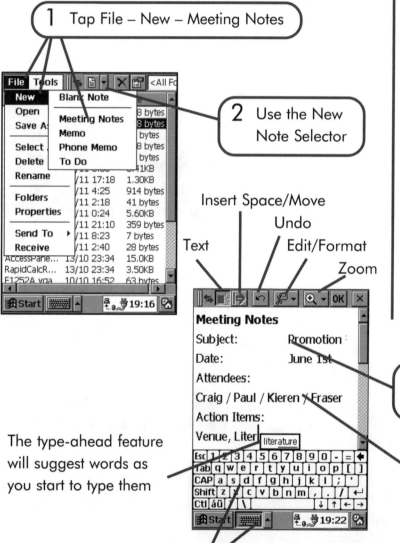

1 Tap File – New – Meeting Notes

2 Use the New Note Selector

Insert Space/Move

Undo

Text

Edit/Format

Zoom

The type-ahead feature will suggest words as you start to type them

4 Tap and type to the right of Subject

5 Add other text

3 Bring up the SIP Keyboard

58

Basic steps

1 Select the Text button (or have the Software Input Panel up).

2 Highlight the text you wish to format.

3 Tap the Edit/Format button.

4 Select Format....

5 Tap the drop-down arrows to select the Font, Size, Line Width or Color.

6 Tap the Bold, Italic, Underline or Strikethrough check boxes to turn the effects on or off.

Tip

If you want to write all your documents in Tahoma 10 point – or whatever settings you have chosen – tap **Set as Default**.

Formatting text

When you have some information on the screen, it's time to try out a few of those other options in Notetaker.

While the software input panel is up (or you have pressed the Text button to get the text cursor), you can highlight text and alter how it looks. You can change its font, size, line width and color, and add emphasis with italics, bold and underline. Strikethrough draws a line through the middle of words – a rarely used effect!

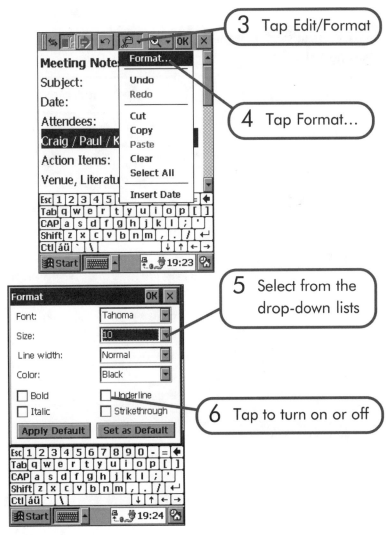

3 Tap Edit/Format

4 Tap Format...

5 Select from the drop-down lists

6 Tap to turn on or off

Handwritten notes

One of the nicest features on Notetaker is the ability to mix both typed text and handwritten notes on the same line or page. Before you insert a handwritten note you might not be sure whether it will fit so you can use the "Space" button to insert some space, then move the typed text back and join it all neatly together again. Here's how.

This method can be applied even on the same line and for both typed and handwritten notes or any combination thereof.

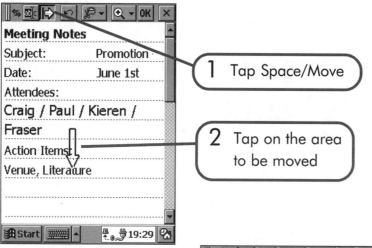

1 Tap Space/Move

2 Tap on the area to be moved

Basic steps

❑ To make space

1 Tap ⏩ the Space/ Move button.

2 Tap and hold the area you want to move down – watch the icon change.

3 Drag downwards a few lines, then release the stylus. You should have some space.

4 Handwrite some text on the screen.

❑ To close up a gap

5 Tap ⏩ the Space/ Move button.

6 Tap the lower text and drag upwards.

Take note

You must use a stylus and press very gently on the screen.

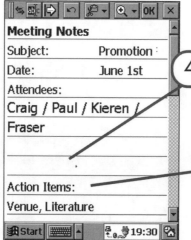

4 Add handwritten notes

3 Drag down to make space

Saving your Note

1 Tap a note to select it.

2 Tap 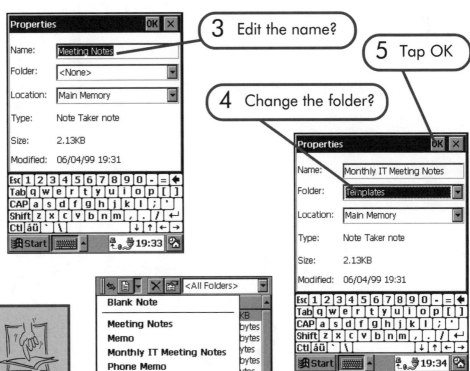 the Properties button.

3 Edit or retype the name to rename it.

or

4 Select a new folder.

5 Tap OK.

If you tap OK when you have finished your note, Notetaker will save it for you, but giving it a name such as **Meeting Note(1)** or **(2)** etc. If you want a note to have a more meaningful name, either use the File Save As command when you have finished writing it, or rename it afterwards.

In the main Notetaker window you can rename your notes, move them to separate folders or turn them into templates.

3 Edit the name?

5 Tap OK

4 Change the folder?

Properties | OK | ×

Name: Meeting Notes
Folder: <None>
Location: Main Memory
Type: Note Taker note
Size: 2.13KB
Modified: 06/04/99 19:31

Properties | OK | ×

Name: Monthly IT Meeting Notes
Folder: Templates
Location: Main Memory
Type: Note Taker note
Size: 2.13KB
Modified: 06/04/99 19:31

<All Folders>

Blank Note

Meeting Notes
Memo
Monthly IT Meeting Notes
Phone Memo
To Do

comdex fri...	16/11 17:18	1.30KB
Bill gates k...	16/11 4:25	914 bytes
comdex fri...	16/11 2:18	41 bytes
Comdex ho...	15/11 0:24	5.60KB
Arrived at c...	12/11 21:10	359 bytes
2264	11/11 8:23	7 bytes
Cserve vegas	11/11 2:40	28 bytes
AccessPane...	13/10 23:34	15.0KB
RapidCalcR...	13/10 23:34	3.50KB

Start | 19:35

After Monthly IT Meeting Notes has been saved in the Templates folder (above), it is added to the New Note list as a template (left).

Summary

❑ Using folders lets you keep your documents organized and can save you time when searching for one.

❑ Pocket Word on Handheld PC devices has lots of options including changing fonts, displaying text in various styles, bulleted and numbered lists and a spell checker.

❑ Copying and pasting is easily done.

❑ The Zoom mode lets you view your document close up, and from a distance.

❑ Creating Templates for commonly typed documents can save you quite a lot of time.

❑ In the Palm-size PCs, explore Notetaker's keyboard/hardware shortcuts.

❑ Notetaker notes can include both handwritten and typed text.

❑ You can move text and handwritten notes around within Notetaker.

❑ Notes can be renamed or saved in other folders.

❑ Saving a note in the Templates folder turns it into a template.

Tip

Notetaker on the Palm-size PCs can read desktop word processed documents in Rich Text Format. I've loaded a 500Kb file into Notetaker.

5 Finances and money

Microsoft Pocket Excel

You can keep track of your expenses and perform other calculations with Microsoft Pocket Excel. There are also a number of third-party software packages available for mobile devices. These will all allow you to synchronize with desktop applications like Microsoft Money, Intuit's Quicken or Quicken Expensable.

Pocket Excel has the look and feel of the desktop version – the formulas work in the same way and it has the most commonly used features, including over 100 functions.

Creating an Excel workbook

The example below is for Fraser's Monitor Shop, which sells computer monitors and LCD flat panels of various shapes and sizes. The spreadsheet is used to let him see at a glance how many monitors and LCD flat panels people have on order and when his customers can expect to receive them.

Tip

If you hold the stylus down on a button, it will show you the description for the button and its keyboard shortcut.

Take note

Pocket Excel is only available on the Hand-held PC range.

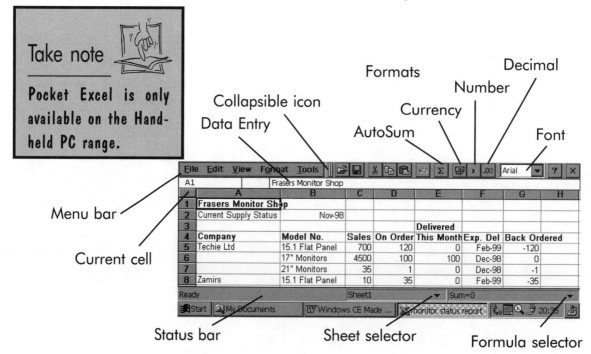

Formats

Decimal

Number

Currency

AutoSum

Font

Collapsible icon

Data Entry

Menu bar

Current cell

Status bar

Sheet selector

Formula selector

Workbooks and templates

1 Double-tap on the Pocket Excel icon.

or

2 Tap Start – Programs – Office – Microsoft Pocket Excel.

3 Tap File – New – Workbook from Template.

4 Select *Expense Report* and tap OK.

5 To enter text or a formula, tap on a cell and type in the Data entry area.

❑ Formatting

6 Tap the Collapsible icon to open the full formatting toolbar.

7 Tap the cell, or a row or column header to select a full line, then tap the formatting buttons as required.

The built-in templates use some of Excel's great features – well worth looking at. In this next example we will create a workbook from the Expenses Template.

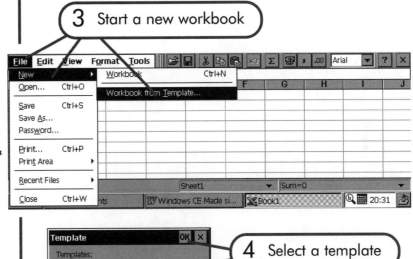

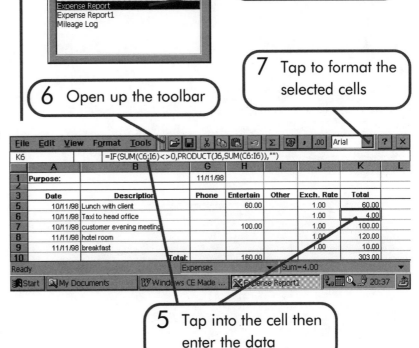

65

Saving a spreadsheet based on a template

When you have entered your data and you wish to save it, tap the Save icon and you will see the Save dialog box displayed. The filename is automatically generated based on the name of the template, but can be edited or replaced by a more meaningful one of your own.

Creating your own Excel templates

A spreadsheet can be turned into a template for future reuse simply by saving it in the Templates folder.

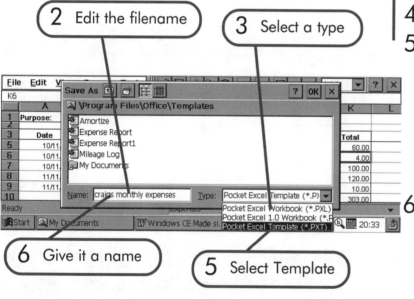

Basic steps

1 Tap 🖫 to open the Save dialog box.

2 Edit the filename if desired.

3 Select the Type of file – *Pocket Excel Workbook* or *Pocket Excel 1.0 file.*

❑ Saving a template

4 Tap File – Save As.

5 In the Save dialog box, change the Type to *Pocket Excel Template.* You should automatically be moved to the Templates folder.

6 Give the file a name. It will be given a *.pxt* extension to indicate it is a Pocket Excel Template.

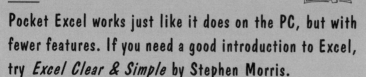

Tip

Pocket Excel works just like it does on the PC, but with fewer features. If you need a good introduction to Excel, try *Excel Clear & Simple* by Stephen Morris.

Pocket Finance

Anyware Consulting Inc. has produced Pocket Finance for both the Handheld and Palm-size PCs. Its features list includes the ability to import and export your data with desktop applications such as Microsoft Money and Intuit Quicken as well as allowing you to have multiple accounts. You can even create an unlimited number of separate accounts – I create a new account for each trip to help separate my expenses. Multiple folders and split expense types are also supported.

The user interface on Pocket Finance is clear and easy to use. It features quick and detailed methods of entering each expense, including a toolbar button, which opens a data entry panel to enter your expense details. It also has a handy icon to bring up the Windows CE calculator.

> **Take note**
>
> Some vendors include Pocket Finance with their mobile devices.

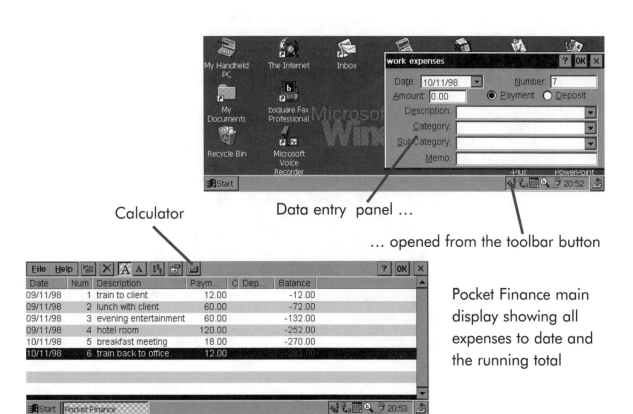

Calculator

Data entry panel ...

... opened from the toolbar button

Pocket Finance main display showing all expenses to date and the running total

Tipster

Have you ever been in a restaurant where a large group of you try to work out how to split the bill 17 ways or you need to work out the tip?

Ilium software has created this application for a quick and easy way to split the bill *x* ways (for instance at a restaurant). It also easily calculates the amount for the tip.

It's nicely customizable and very simply to use. There are versions available for the Handheld PC and the Palm-size PC, I've shown the Handheld PC version here, with the Configure buttons dialog box open. The button options let you select the percentages you wish to allocate for the tip.

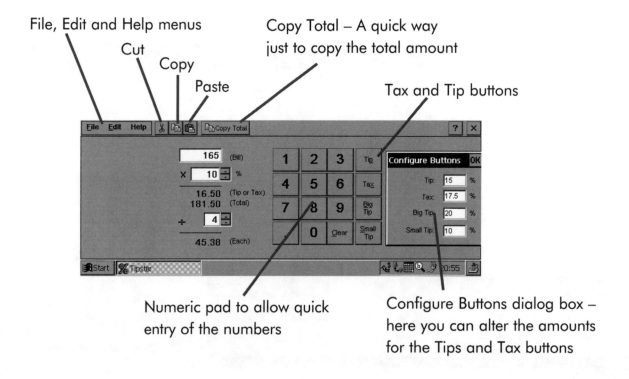

File, Edit and Help menus

Cut

Copy

Paste

Copy Total – A quick way just to copy the total amount

Tax and Tip buttons

Numeric pad to allow quick entry of the numbers

Configure Buttons dialog box – here you can alter the amounts for the Tips and Tax buttons

Calculators

Windows CE comes with a basic calculator as standard but lots of third party software companies have produced financial and more fully featured calculators. Here is a quick overview of the calculator included with Windows CE devices.

File, Edit and View menus

Copy selected data

Paste

Standard/Pop-Up Views

Value Stored in Memory identifier

Backspace (to delete errors)

Clear Entry

Clear all

Memory Clear

Memory Recall

Add to Memory

Store in Memory

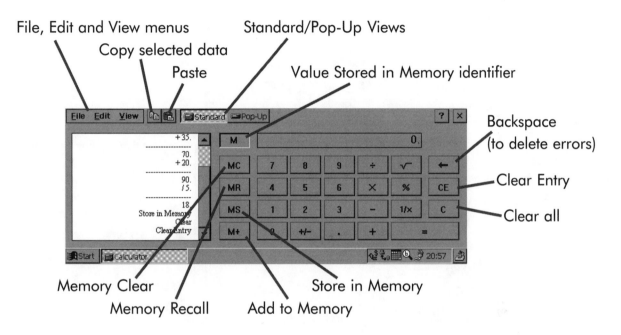

Third party software

Several companies produce financial and programmable calculators. It is outside the scope of this chapter to show all of them, but here are just some of them.

Landware – Financial Consultant

Landware – Fiscal Professional

Applian Technologies – Coolcalc

DeveloperOne – Rapidcalc for the Palm-size PC.

For more details of any of these, check the vendors' Web sites. You will find their addresses at the back of the book.

Storing and securing data

While I showed you how to password protect your device, spreadsheets and Pocket Word documents in earlier chapters, there is a lot of information that you may normally carry around with you in your wallet or purse that you'd like to store in your Windows CE device.

The built-in applications don't offer many features to store password-protected entries for specific data, but some vendors have produced applications that are depositories for miscellaneous but still very important data.

eWallet

eWallet from Ilium Software is marketed as an Electronic Wallet. It supports such features as password protecting sections, hide/show pin numbers on card details, as well as standard cards for common activities, and free-form cards so you can enter any details you want.

eWallet has many features including the ability to search for information stored in the wallet. You can also change how the card is displayed, either on the left or the right.

When you lock the wallet by pressing the Lock Icon, any sections that you have password protected will need the password entered before you can view the information.

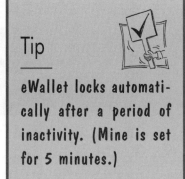

Tip

eWallet locks automatically after a period of inactivity. (Mine is set for 5 minutes.)

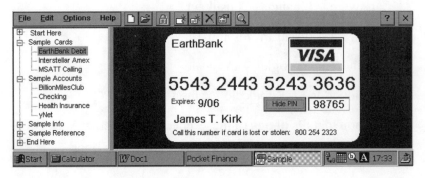

eWallet from Ilium Software – information is stored on cards, organized into folders

I use eWallet to store all the pieces of information I used to store on scraps of paper or on cards in my wallet. Some of the information I store in eWallet include details of my telephone calling card, how to access work's voice mail, medical numbers, emergency numbers to call if I lose my credit cards and other such details. I even keep the numbers of local taxis, restaurants and favorite wine bars.

QuickWallet

Applian Technologies has created QuickWallet, a product conceptually similar to Ilium's eWallet, in that information is stored on cards, organized into sections and categories.

QuickWallet has the ability to have information password protected. Its major differences from eWallet are that its buttons for finding information are very large, so it's possible to navigate really quickly (even without using the stylus). It's also possible to keep track of images, audio files and telephone numbers from within QuickWallet. If you store phone numbers in the application you can even get your mobile device to dial the numbers for you – just hold up the speaker to a phone and it dials! The application uses multiple levels for sections, and then cards, allowing you to store a lot of information and retrieve it quickly and easily. QuickWallet is available on both Handheld and Palm-size PCs.

Summary

❏ Pocket Excel is a powerful spreadsheet application with all the key features of the desktop version, including over a hundred functions.

❏ You can save templates based on any of your existing Pocket Excel spreadsheets.

❏ Pocket Finance lets you keep track of your expenses. Versions are available for all Windows CE devices.

❏ Ever stuck at the end of an evening out trying to split the bill and work out the tip? Tipster from Ilium Software handles this task admirably.

❏ The Windows CE built-in calculator is very basic. Lots of third-party developers offer more powerful ones.

❏ If you find yourself carrying around lots of scraps of paper and business cards, then secure data storage applications such as those from Ilium or Applian can help you out.

6 Communications

CE Services

When you purchase a Windows CE device you get some software from Microsoft to load onto your desktop PC – Windows CE Services. Its main job is to keep the data on your PC synchronized with the data on your mobile device.

Use CE Services to back up your device, copy files between your PC and mobile device and connect a network adapter to speed up those tasks. CE Services can also convert documents, spreadsheets and other files from desktop to the more compact mobile device format.

Windows CE services is a very powerful application but it is incredibly easy to use – so much of the work is done automatically and behind the scenes, that you hardly need to think about it. It allows mobile devices to connect to your PC with a variety of options – a serial cable is the most common and is supplied with your mobile device. It also supports connection from a network card, if present in your mobile device (see page 77).

Take note

Mobile devices vary. For instructions on connecting your device to a PC, see the manufacturer's documentation that came with it.

Mobile Devices, part of Windows CE services, running on a desktop PC

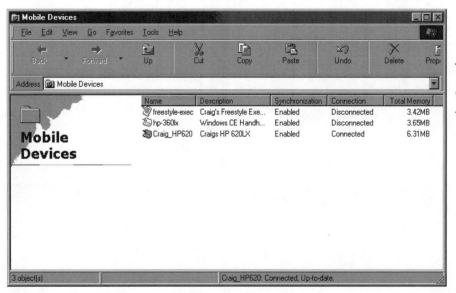

This example has connections set up for three different mobile devices.

Basic steps

1 Connect your device and PC and run CE Services.

2 Open the Tools menu.

3 Select Backup/Restore.

4 Select an option – *Backup* or *Restore* – then tap OK.

or

5 Click Tools and select Back Up Now.

6 If desired, change the folder or name of the backup file by selecting the browse button.

7 Click OK to start the backup.

Backing up

One task often overlooked with all computer systems is the backing up of your data. A Windows CE device can be easily backed up on the PC. If you ever accidentally lose some of your data or have your mobile device stolen, then having a backup handy will save lots of time and frustration.

There are several backup options. I have my machine set to perform an incremental backup, so that it only copies the data that has changed since the last backup. It makes it quick.

I recommend you back up your device at least once a week – quite a lot of people I know have the option set to back up every time they connect to their PC. It will depend on your working practices as to how often you want to back up your device.

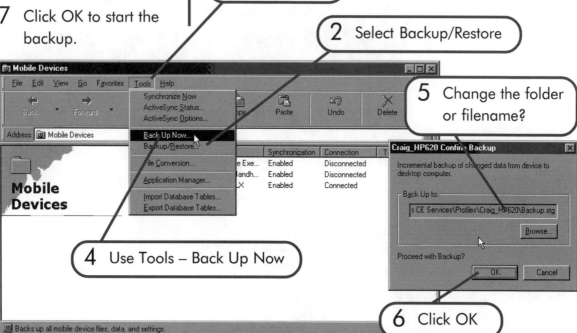

1 Click Tools

2 Select Backup/Restore

5 Change the folder or filename?

4 Use Tools – Back Up Now

6 Click OK

Restoring a backup

In the unlikely event that you need to restore a backup, the only restore option available in CE Services is to restore the whole machine. As this erases all the data currently on the device, you will be asked to confirm the operation before it starts.

Basic steps

1 Tap Tools.

2 Tap Backup/Restore.

3 Tap Restore.

4 Select the backup you wish to restore.

5 Tap OK.

6 Tap the Restore button.

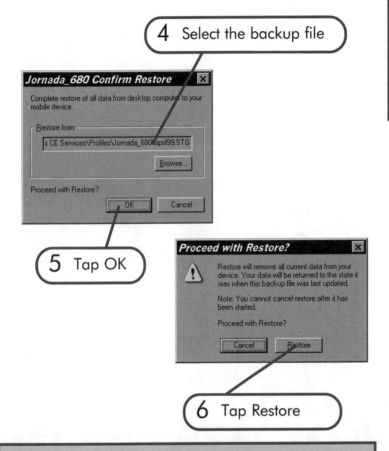

4 Select the backup file

Jornada_680 Confirm Restore

Complete restore of all data from desktop computer to your mobile device.

Restore from:

`s CE Services\Profiles\Jornada_680\april99.STG`

Browse...

Proceed with Restore?

OK   Cancel

5 Tap OK

Proceed with Restore?

Restore will remove all current data from your device. Your data will be returned to the state it was when this backup file was last updated.

Note: You cannot cancel restore after it has been started.

Proceed with Restore?

Cancel   Restore

6 Tap Restore

Take note

If you change your country settings then you will get an error when you try to restore. If you backed up with UK settings and try to restore with USA settings you'll get an error, change the country back to UK in the control panel to rectify this anomaly.

Tip

Anyware Consulting (http://hometown.aol.com/anyware) has created an application, Anyware Consulting H/PC Vault, that will allow you to restore individual files from your backup files and put them back onto your mobile device.

Using an Ethernet card

By using an Ethernet card (also called a network card) with your Windows CE device it's possible to synchronize with your PC and access corporate data and printers at much higher speeds than if you are directly connected to your PC with a serial cable.

First check that the network card is supported in your CE device. All manufacturers have a list of supported products. Mine is a Socket LP-E (Low Power Ethernet), an NE2000 compatible PCMCIA Type II adapter, from Socket Communications.

Most Handheld PCs and PC Pros have the networking drivers already loaded on them. If your machine doesn't, then please refer to the Microsoft CD-ROM that came with your mobile device, it should contain the drivers and they should also be on a driver diskette or CD-ROM that came with your network card.

A lot of computer departments have particular rules and guidelines for connecting devices up to the corporate network, so always seek the assistance of a member of that department when dealing with network issues. First check that there is an available port for your Ethernet connection and that it operates at the same speed as the adapter for your mobile device. You should also ask if they support DHCP (Dynamic Host Configuration Protocol) and if you have a WINS (Windows Internet Name Service) Server on your network. DHCP and WINS servers will greatly simplify the task of connecting your H/PC up to the network.

> **Take note**
>
> You can also use wireless Ethernet adapter cards such as those made by Proxim. Drivers for both these cards are supplied as standard on the Handheld PC Pro which makes setting up really easy.

The setup dialog that appears when you first plug in an Ethernet card

77

Setting up Ethernet connections

Let's begin configuring our system. I'll be covering the easy way and then the method that covers all the little details that you may need if you are experiencing problems.

Once you have set up the ActiveSync, you will be connected to your PC and will be able to perform nearly all Windows CE Services features much more quickly.

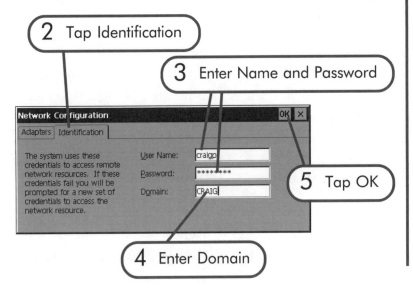

1   Insert the Ethernet card into your H/PC.

2   Tap the Identification tab.

3   Enter your User Name and Password for the machine you'll be synchronizing with.

4   Enter the Domain name if required.

5   Tap OK.

❑   To connect to your PC

6   Tap Start – Programs – Communications and select ActiveSync.

7   If the information is correct tap Connect.

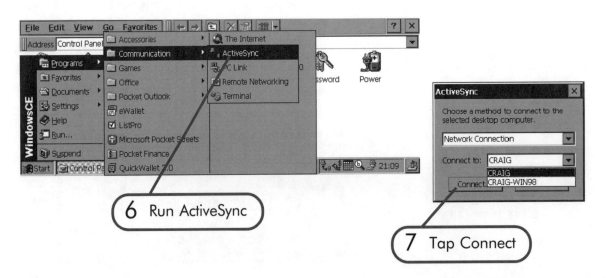

Basic steps

1 Tap Start, Settings then Control Panel.

2 Double-tap the Network Icon.

3 Select the adapter type and tap Properties.

4 For a fixed IP Address, tap Specify an IP Address and enter the IP Address and the Subnet Mask. Leave the Default Gateway blank unless told otherwise.

5 Tap the Name Servers tab.

6 Enter the numbers for the Primary WINS Server.

7 Tap OK, and again at the Network window.

Manual setup

You need to find out, then enter into your CE machine:

● The IP Address of your PC (the one with CE Services).

● Your network's Subnet Mask and Default Gateway.

● IP Address of any WINS Server or DNS Servers if used.

● Whether your CE device will use a fixed IP address or whether it will be allocated a number each time using a method called DHCP. If using a fixed IP Address you will need to get the number from the IT department.

● The port on your network to connect your device to.

● The user name and password to the PC you wish to access.

● Your machine's network name, which could be something obscure like LDN00061 or your name – it depends how the computer or IT department set up your PC.

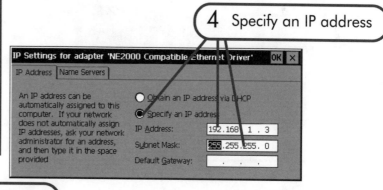

4 Specify an IP address

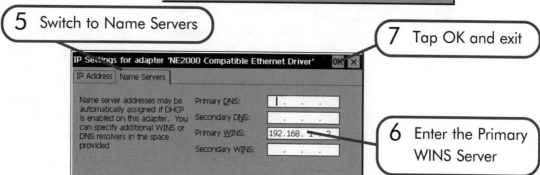

5 Switch to Name Servers

7 Tap OK and exit

6 Enter the Primary WINS Server

Making the connection

When you have worked through the steps, you will be connected to your PC at very high speed.

On the PC try backing up your device and select a full backup, it should take about 1 minute to back up 8Mb-worth of data!

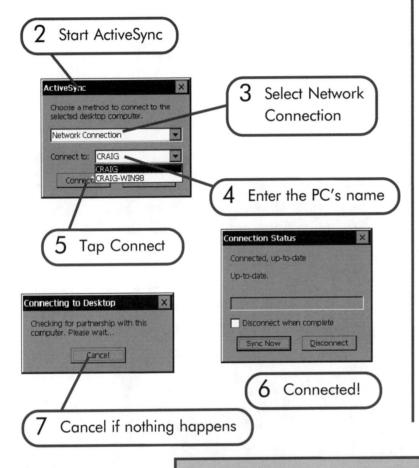

2 Start ActiveSync

ActiveSync
Choose a method to connect to the selected desktop computer.
Network Connection
Connect to: CRAIG
CRAIG
CRAIG-WIN98

3 Select Network Connection

4 Enter the PC's name

5 Tap Connect

Connecting to Desktop
Checking for partnership with this computer. Please wait...
Cancel

Connection Status
Connected, up-to-date
Up-to-date.
☐ Disconnect when complete
Sync Now   Disconnect

6 Connected!

7 Cancel if nothing happens

Basic steps

1 Plug in the Network Adapter.

2 Tap Start – Programs – Communications – ActiveSync.

3 Tap the drop-down box and select Network Connection.

4 In the Connect to: box, enter the name of your PC.

5 Tap Connect.

6 You should see a box saying *Checking partnership* and then the Connection Status box should appear.

7 If the Connection Status box has not opened after a few minutes, tap Cancel and check the set up.

Tip

As network cards use a lot of power it is best to always use an AC adapter when you want to use network cards in your mobile device.

Shared network drives

1 Tap Start – Programs
– Windows Explorer.

2 In the Address Field
type *machinename*
(replace this with the
actual name!) and hit
[Enter] – this will show
you all the shared
folders on that com-
puter.

3 To navigate to a par-
ticular share double-
tap on its name.

or

4 Browse it until you find
the required folder or
share that you are
trying to connect to.

Once you have your Windows CE device connected to the
network you can easily access other network resources such as
shared drives. To be able to connect to the network share you
will need to know the name of the resource or the name of the
machine it is on.

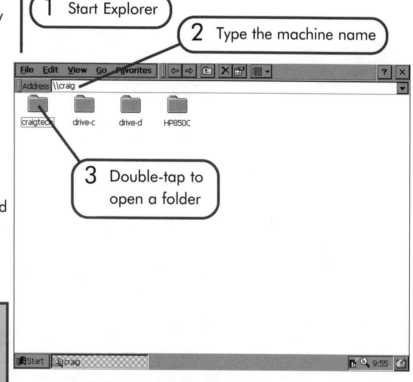

1 Start Explorer

2 Type the machine name

3 Double-tap to
open a folder

File   Edit   View   Go   Favorites

Address \\craig

craigtec   drive-c   drive-d   HP850C

Start   craig   9:55

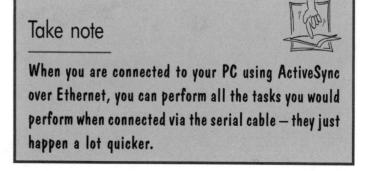

Tip

You can go directly to the
share by typing its name
after the machine name in
the form:

\ \machine\sharename

Take note

When you are connected to your PC using ActiveSync
over Ethernet, you can perform all the tasks you would
perform when connected via the serial cable – they just
happen a lot quicker.

Copying files from network drives

When you are connected to the drive in question and you are in the required folder, copying files is simple, but otherwise all you need to do is change to the right folder first.

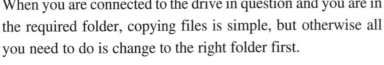

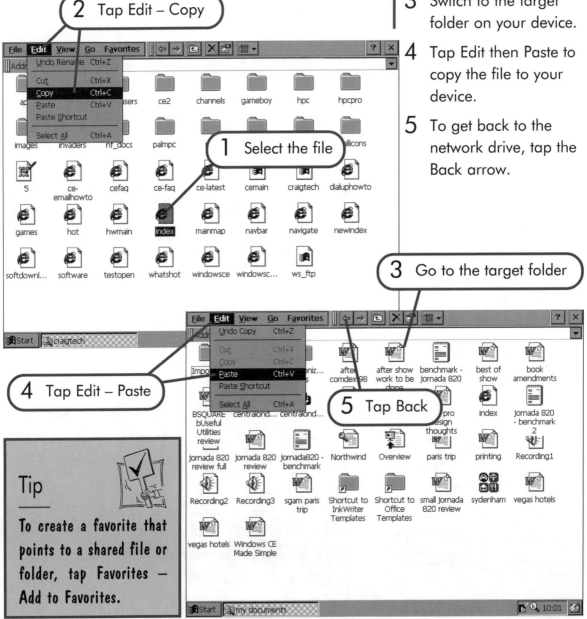

Basic steps

1 Highlight the file by tapping on it once.

2 Tap Edit then Copy.

3 Switch to the target folder on your device.

4 Tap Edit then Paste to copy the file to your device.

5 To get back to the network drive, tap the Back arrow.

Tip

To create a favorite that points to a shared file or folder, tap Favorites – Add to Favorites.

Network printing

❑ Printing from Word

1 Open up or type a new document in Pocket Word.

2 Tap File – Print.

3 Select the Printer and the Port.

4 Type the Net Path – this will normally take the form:
*PCname**printername*

5 Select the Paper size.

6 Change other settings as required.

7 Tap OK.

Once you have your Windows CE device connected to your network it is possible to print to any of the network printers you have shared access to.

I have an ink jet printer connected to my PC and it's shared. Here is how you configure it to print from the mobile device.

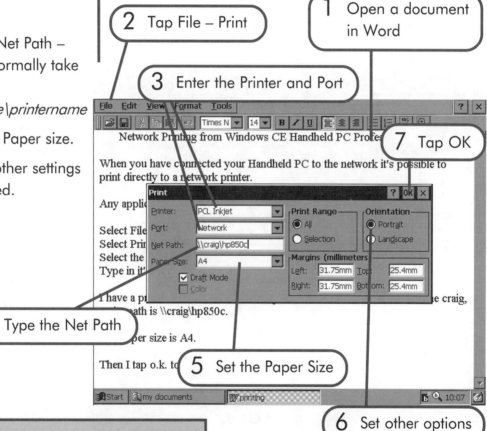

2 Tap File – Print

1 Open a document in Word

3 Enter the Printer and Port

7 Tap OK

4 Type the Net Path

5 Set the Paper Size

6 Set other options

Take note

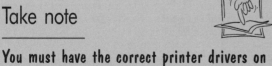

You must have the correct printer drivers on your CE device to print documents correctly.

Fax software

A lot of hardware vendors include BSQUARE Development's bFAX software. This software (when used with a modem) turns your Windows CE device into a fax machine.

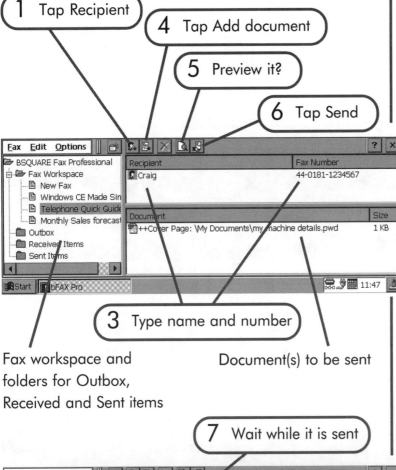

1 Tap Recipient

4 Tap Add document

5 Preview it?

6 Tap Send

3 Type name and number

Fax workspace and folders for Outbox, Received and Sent items

Document(s) to be sent

7 Wait while it is sent

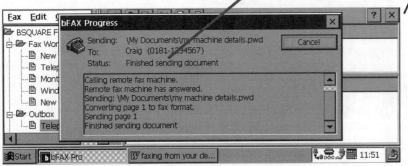

- To send a fax

1 Tap Recipient 🔲.

2 Tap the Contacts button and select one from the list.

or

3 Type in the name of the recipient and the number – the area and country code will be picked up from your dialing preferences.

4 Tap Add document 🔲 and double-tap the document you want to send.

5 If you want to check it, tap Preview 🔲 and use the scroll bars and zoom to look it over.

6 Tap Send fax 🔲.

7 Watch and wait for the Finished message.

Faxes from Pocket Word

1 Tap the File menu and select Print.

2 For the Printer, select Print-to-bFAX.

3 Set the other options as required.

4 Tap OK.

5 The document will be passed to bFAX for you to select your recipient before sending the fax.

All Windows computers treat fax software as a type of printer, allowing you to send a fax directly from a word-processor or other application. Here's how to send a fax from Pocket Word.

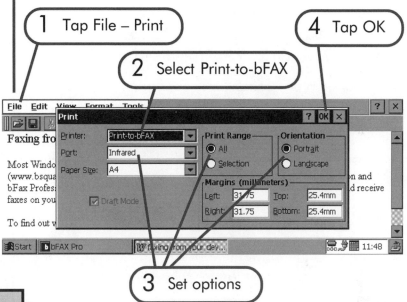

1 Tap File – Print

2 Select Print-to-bFAX

4 Tap OK

3 Set options

Tip

There are options on the View menu to make it easier to read an incoming fax. Use Rotate Fax or Inverse Fax to turn the message the right way round, and Zoom in as close as you need to be able to see the details.

Take note

bFax Lite, which is included on some machines, does not have the ability to receive faxes, for that you'll need bFAX Professional.

Summary

❏ Every Windows CE device comes with CE Services, which is used to connect your PC with your device and is the main method of synchronizing your data with your PC.

❏ When your PC is connected to your device you can perform backups, install new software or copy files and information to or from your device.

❏ Backing up any computer is important. You can run the CE Services backup from within the Mobile Devices program on your PC.

❏ If you have a network card in your device you can connect to other network machines and copy files at high speed as well as perform functions that you would normally do over a serial cable.

❏ When configuring a network card, check with your IT department to get the machine details for your servers.

❏ Before you try to print to a network printer from a Windows CE device, check that your printer driver matches the printer or else your documents may not print correctly.

❏ If you want to send and receive faxes on your device, you'll need a package like bFax Professional.

❏ You can send a fax through the Print routine in any application.

7 Getting online

Connecting to the Internet

Before you can connect your Handheld PC to the Internet you will need the following:

- A modem and phone line.

- An Internet Service Provider (ISP).

- The modem phone number of your Internet provider.

- Your login details – login name and password.

- Your ISP's Domain Name Server (DNS) settings. To get this information you may have to call your Internet provider's technical support department.

To enable you to connect to the Internet from your Handheld PC you will need to use Remote Networking.

Having connected to several different ISPs, I have found that there are slight differences in how the connection actually works, so if the first method doesn't work for you don't despair, the second method should get you connected.

Take note

Although most PCMCIA modems work with Handheld PCs, to ensure compatibility you should check with your hardware vendor.

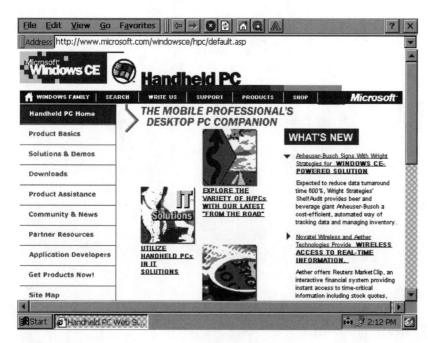

1 Tap Start – Programs – Communications and then Remote Networking.

2 Double-tap Make New Connection.

3 Enter a Name for the connection.

4 Select Dial-Up Connection and tap Next.

5 At the Select a modem connection panel, select the modem and click the Configure button.

...cont

Some devices come with a built-in modem, with those devices you'll just have to plug the phone line into the wall.

To set up the hardware, switch off the H/PC, plug in the modem, switch on the H/PC and plug in AC power.

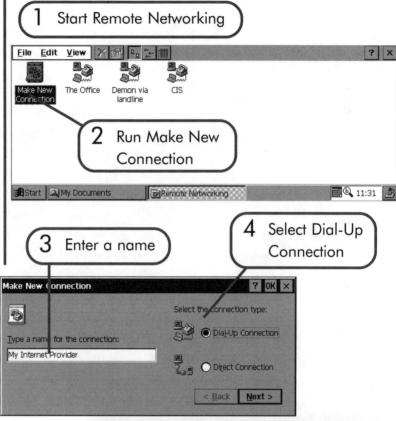

1 Start Remote Networking

2 Run Make New Connection

3 Enter a name

4 Select Dial-Up Connection

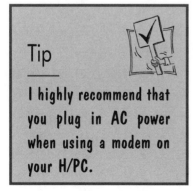

Tip

I highly recommend that you plug in AC power when using a modem on your H/PC.

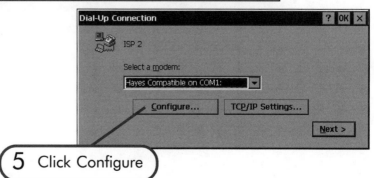

5 Click Configure

89

...cont

6 Set the highest Baud rate

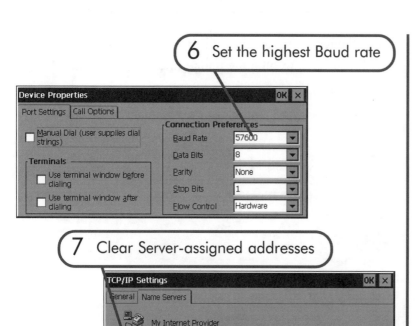

7 Clear Server-assigned addresses

8 Enter your DNS numbers

9 Enter the phone number and tap Finish

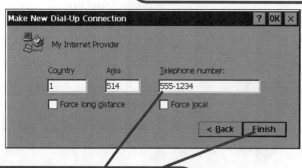

6 At the Port Settings, make sure that the Baud rate is set to the highest your modem can manage. Leave the rest at their defaults and tap OK.

7 Tap TCP/IP Settings and on the Name Servers tab uncheck the Server-assigned addresses field.

8 Enter the Primary and secondary DNS numbers (your ISP will tell you these).

9 Check the details, entering the telephone number of your ISP if it wasn't picked up earlier, and tap Finish.

Take note

DNS entries identify computers on the Internet. Fortunately, most of them also have names, such as www.microsoft.com which can be used when browsing.

Basic steps

1 Double-tap on the icon for your new connection.

2 Enter your User Name for your ISP.

3 Enter your Password.

4 Check the Phone number and Dial from and tap Connect.

5 When the connection is completed, tap Hide to remove the message box. You can now do such things as e-mail and Web browsing.

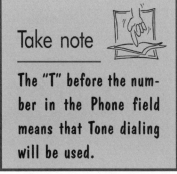

Take note

The "T" before the number in the Phone field means that Tone dialing will be used.

Testing the connection

Here is where it can sometimes go wrong! If you get connected and then after a short time period (usually 15–20 seconds) the line drops, then check out the next section for advice.

If you don't get "User Authenticated" then the login didn't complete properly.

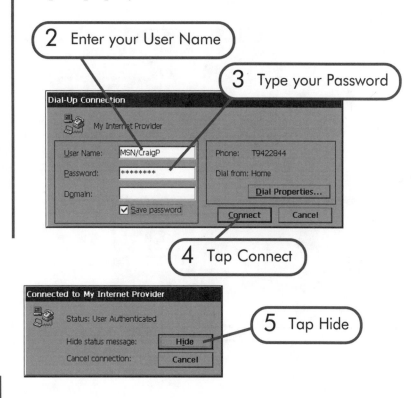

I'm lucky enough to have an ISP (Internet Service Provider) that supports Microsoft PAP/CHAP user authentication, which simplifies logging in from a Windows computer. The user name and password entered into the dialog boxes are passed to the ISP when I dial in and I'm logged in quickly and efficiently.

Manual login

If your service provider doesn't support MS PAP/CHAP user authentication, you will have to log in manually.

Your TCP/IP settings will be different. Every ISP has its own unique DNS numbers, and some assign these automatically – tick Server-assigned IP address for these. Check with your provider!

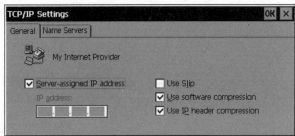

Server-assigned addresses?

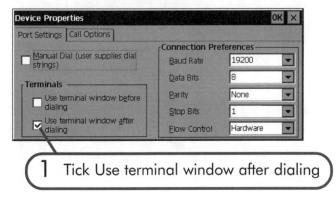

1 Tick Use terminal window after dialing

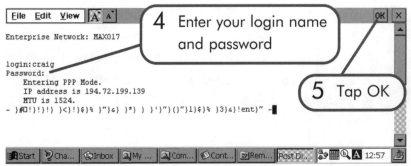

4 Enter your login name and password

5 Tap OK

❑ Setting up

1 Follow the steps on pages 89 to 90, but at the Device Properties dialog box, check Use terminal window after dialing.

❑ Logging in

2 Double-tap on your connection icon.

3 Don't enter anything in the User Name and Password Fields, just tap Connect.

4 You will usually be presented with a blank screen, press [Enter] then log in with your username and password at the prompts.

5 Tap the OK button in the top right-hand corner when you see "garbage" appear (it's just the connection working).

Basic steps

1 Double-tap on the Internet Explorer icon on the desktop.

2 In Address field type in www.craigtech.co.uk then press [Enter].

3 To move up and down this page tap the vertical scroll bar.

4 If the page is too wide then tap the horizontal scroll bar.

Pocket Internet Explorer

On Windows CE Handheld PCs, the program for browsing the Web is Pocket Internet Explorer. If you are familiar with Internet Explorer on the desktop PC, this will look familiar.

Over the next few pages you'll learn how to visit Web sites, search the Internet, save your favorite sites for easy access later, and change some of the Internet Explorer settings.

Visiting a Web site

Here's how to visit my site. First use your dial-up connection to get onto the Internet, then follow the steps.

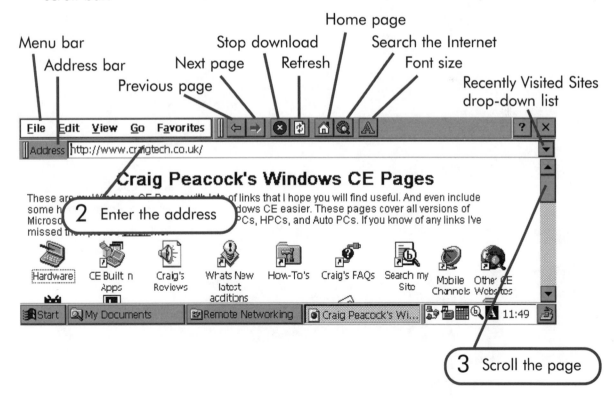

The Favorites folder

Keeping sites in your Favorites folder will save you having to type in the name every time you want to visit it.

As screen space is quite limited, it's a good idea to save sites within folders. That way your screen won't get too cluttered even when you have a large number of favorites. You can create folders and move favorites between them in the Organize Favorites routine. Use the same techniques as you do when managing files and folders in Windows Explorer.

Basic steps

❑ Adding a Favorite

1 Tap Favorites.

2 Tap Add to Favorites.

3 Edit the name if needed then tap OK.

❑ Using Favorites

4 Tap Favorites.

5 Tap a favorite to link to its page.

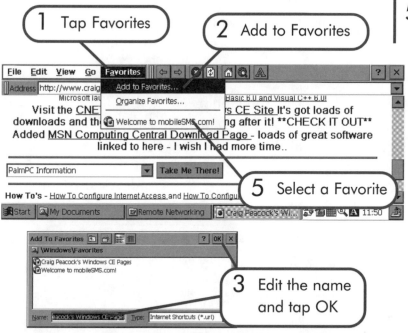

Tip

If the text on a page is too big or too small, tap the Font Size icon until you find a size that suits.

Tip

When you are surfing on a Handheld PC, hold down [Alt] and tap the screen to bring up a menu of options, such as **Open in New Window** and **Save Picture As.** Try it on a graphic or a link.

Internet options

Basic steps

❑ Autodial

1 Tap View – Options – Autodial.

2 Tap the Use Autodial check box to tick it.

3 In the drop-down box, choose your connection.

4 I recommend leaving Auto Disconnect set and set the Disconnect if Idle to 5 or 10 minutes. To change the Idle time either tap the scroll bars or enter the number in the box.

Take note

When you have finished surfing don't forget to disconnect! Double-tap the Connected icon then tap **Disconnect**.

Autodial

Autodial lets you start Pocket Internet Explorer and type in an Internet site's address (URL) then have the H/PC automatically dial up your Internet connection.

Proxy Server

A Proxy Server is software that runs on a network to authorize or deny access to external networks. If you are in any doubt as to whether you need to have this option set contact your computer department or network administrators.

Advanced

It is not advisable to change these settings, as it can lower your security when visiting Internet sites. A couple of options that are handy are:

● **Size of Cache** – This allocates a certain amount of your machine's memory to store information when you visit Internet sites. If you visit a lot of sites and have the memory available then you could increase the amount, though I wouldn't recommend setting it above 25%.

● **Empty Cache now** – If you notice you are running low on memory on your machine, then emptying the cache and reducing its size to under 10% will free up valuable memory.

Mobile channels

When you browse the Internet you have to go and find the information you want. Channels offer a different approach, using "push technology." If a site offers a channel, you can subscribe to it. When you next go online, the site will push its latest information to you, without you having to visit. Subscribing to channels is usually very easy as Web site owners normally include a channel icon for you to click on.

Mobile channels let you view Web pages on your mobile device, offline. I'll focus on the mobile channels on the Palm-size device here, as all of those devices have the mobile channels viewer installed as standard. The Handheld PC version of the software is now available via a download from the Microsoft Web site.

Channel data is downloaded into your PC and then transferred to the device via ActiveSync when you connect it up. Before data is transferred, ActiveSync must be enabled.

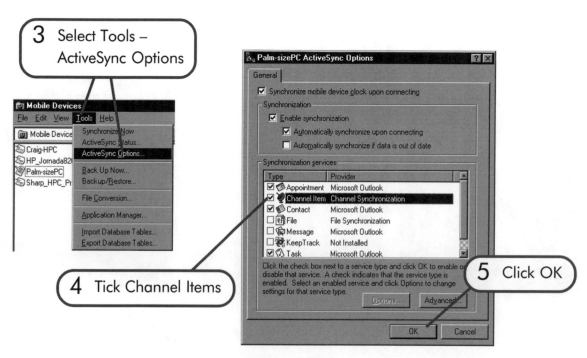

3 Select Tools –
ActiveSync Options

4 Tick Channel Items

5 Click OK

Basic steps

1 Run Internet Explorer on your PC.

2 Connect to your Internet provider.

3 Enter the address: www.palmpc.org.uk/ channels

4 Click the Add Mobile Channel button.

5 The default option to have content auto-matically updated is the best way to keep your content up to date. Just click OK.

cont...

Tip

If you find you aren't looking at a channel that often, unsubscribe to it. You can always re-subscribe to it later.

Adding a channel

Now you've told Windows CE services on the PC that you would like to transfer mobile channels to your mobile device, here's how to add a channel and subscribe to it.

From your PC, you are going to visit a Web site, subscribe to a mobile channel and then transfer it to your mobile device for reading at your leisure.

3 Go to Palm-Size PC Mobile Channels

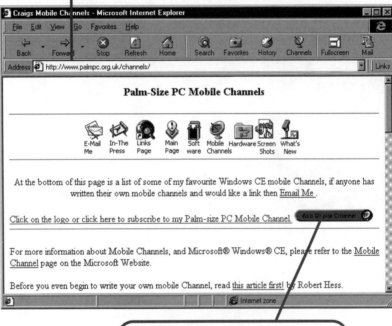

4 Click Add Mobile Channel

5 Click OK

...cont

The Internet Explorer screen after downloading the latest update from my channel, PalmPC. The data is now ready for transfer to a mobile device for offline, offsite reading.

6 You should now see a Channels bar on the left with the icon of my channel. The channel will be updating.

7 When it says *Update complete* you can disconnect from the Internet if you wish.

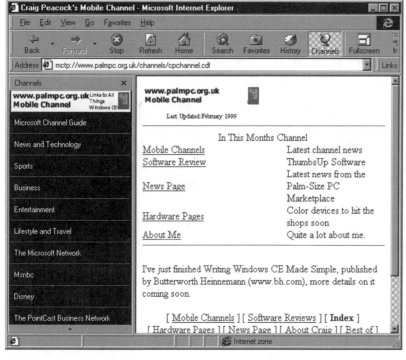

Take note

Channels are most commonly found at news sites. Some sites' channels have several distinct sections, of which you might only be interested in a few. Don't worry, you don't have to download stuff you don't want. Channels allow you to pick the parts that you are interested in.

Basic steps

1 Connect your Windows CE device to the PC. Windows CE Services should open automatically and copy the channel data to your device.

2 On the device itself you should now see the 🌐 icon.

3 Double-tap 🌐 to open the Mobile Channels Viewer.

4 To view a channel double-tap its icon or its entry on the channels home page.

5 To navigate around these pages tap on the underlined text to jump to other pages.

6 To get back a page tap the Back arrow.

7 To return to the menu of subscribed channels tap the Home icon.

Viewing channels on the Palm-size PC

Transferring channel data to a mobile device is a simple, and largely automatic, process. Once it has been copied across, you can browse it at your leisure.

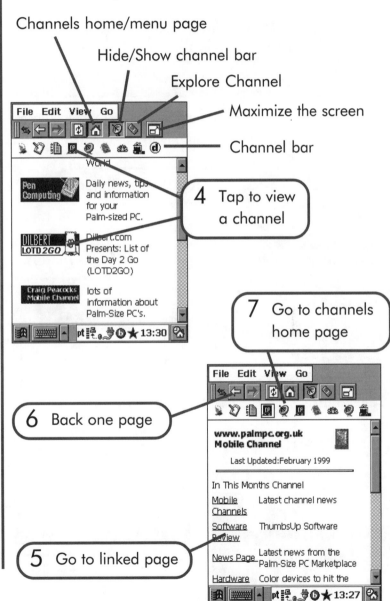

Channels home/menu page

Hide/Show channel bar

Explore Channel

Maximize the screen

Channel bar

4 Tap to view a channel

7 Go to channels home page

6 Back one page

5 Go to linked page

Memory space

When you have already subscribed to several channels and you try to add another you may see this message appear when synchronizing:

It means your device does not have enough memory to allocate for the mobile channel you are trying to subscribe to.

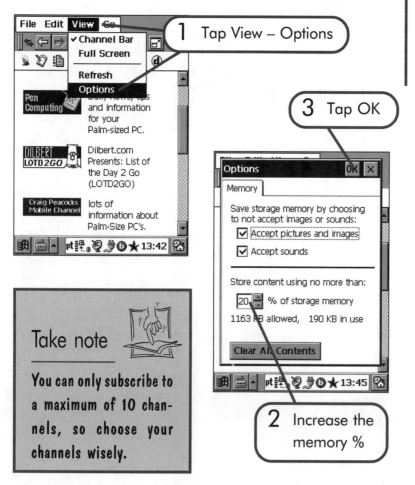

1 Tap View – Options

3 Tap OK

2 Increase the memory %

Basic steps

1 Tap View – Options.

2 Increase the amount of memory available for storing content. Note the allowed and in use amounts, as these will guide you when allocating space.

3 Tap OK.

4 After allocating more space, you will need to re-synchronize with your PC.

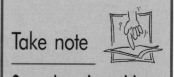

Take note

You can only subscribe to a maximum of 10 channels, so choose your channels wisely.

Take note

Some channels send lots of graphics, increasing the download time and storage needs. If you can opt not to download graphics, it's well worth considering. You can also choose not to copy graphics to your mobile device.

Basic steps

❑ On the PC

1 Run Internet Explorer.

2 Click on the Channels button.

3 Select the channel you want to delete.

4 Right-click on it and select Delete.

5 Click Yes to confirm. The channel is then deleted from your PC.

Deleting a channel

If you find that you don't want a mobile channel copied to your device anymore then it's possible to delete it.

When you want to delete a channel you need to decide if you want to keep the content you have on your device and don't want to update it, or if you want to get rid of the content and not subscribe to it anymore.

In the first example, if you want to keep the current channel content on the device then you need to delete it on the PC.

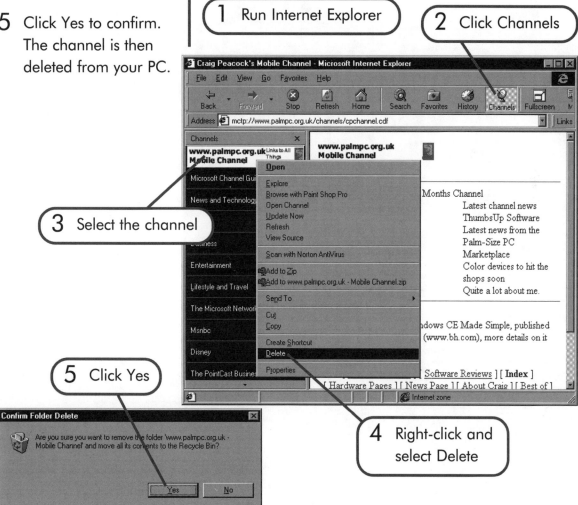

1 Run Internet Explorer

2 Click Channels

3 Select the channel

5 Click Yes

4 Right-click and select Delete

Basic steps

1 Run Mobile Channels

3 Tap File – Channels

4 Clear the check box

5 Tap OK

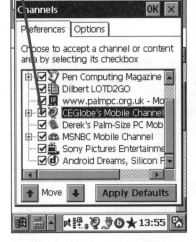

6 Tap Yes

1 Open up the Mobile Channel Viewer.

2 Tap the slider bar to reveal the menu.

3 Tap File then tap Channels.

4 Your channels are listed on the Preferences tab. Untick the check box beside the channel to be deleted.

5 At the confirmation dialog box tap OK.

6 Tap Yes to leave the Channels screen. The data will be deleted and you are back to the Channels home screen.

Channels on Handheld PCs

A mobile channel viewer for the Handheld PCs is available for download from the Microsoft Web site at:

http://www.microsoft.com/windowsce/default.asp

It works just like the Palm-size PC version, only instead of having a separate "home" or main page, the channels are shown on the left of the screen.

All the other features are the same. You conveniently and easily synchronize the channels you are interested in and they get copied to the Handheld PC.

Tip

For the latest news about mobile channels, surf over to my Palm-PC site at www.palmpc.org.uk

Navigation buttons

Explore Channels button – tap to hide the left-hand pane

Channel bar

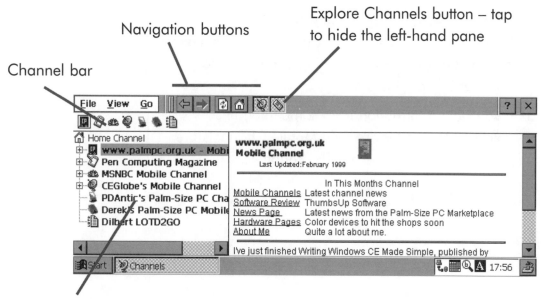

The Channels that you are subscribed to

Summary

❑ Connecting your Windows CE machine to the Internet can sometimes be a little tricky.

❑ Some modems can make your machine's batteries get very low very quickly, always try and use a power supply when using a modem on your device.

❑ Every Internet Service Provider is different. Some of them support automatic logins from Windows CE devices, others don't.

❑ Once you have connected your device to the Internet, you can browse the Web with Microsoft Pocket Internet Explorer.

❑ When you've found sites you want to return to regularly, you can store links to them as Favorites. Favorites can be given more meaningful names and organized into folders.

❑ If you want information from some Internet sites delivered to your device then Mobile Channels are the key. Not all Web sites offer channels.

8 E-mail

Inbox

Inbox is the e-mail application in Windows CE. While it works almost identically on all versions of Windows CE, Inbox has been enhanced and changed over the years since it first came out. I'll highlight the differences with Inbox on each of the platforms as I proceed through the chapter.

How Inbox works

Inbox on mobile devices works as an extension of your PC Inbox, and not a replacement. When you download e-mail messages onto your Windows CE device you are actually downloading a copy of your messages – the originals are still there on the mail server. In contrast, when you connect up with your PC and read e-mail it will download the messages and not leave any on the server.

Inbox on the Handheld PC Pro

All the features that appear on devices running the Windows CE Handheld PC edition are also on the machines that run the Handheld PC Pro edition. The Professional edition has a few more options and lots of new features as well, and over the next few pages you'll see them as you work through some common tasks.

Inbox on the Handheld PC Pro looks a little bit different from the version on the Handheld PC. There are a great number of features that are shared with its earlier version but it has evolved to make some tasks even easier. I'll show you those changes as we progress through this chapter.

Tip
___

If you do not have a modem but you want to be able to read and reply to e-mails, Inbox can be integrated with Microsoft Outlook on your desktop PC.

Inbox on the Handheld PC
(Windows CE 2.0)

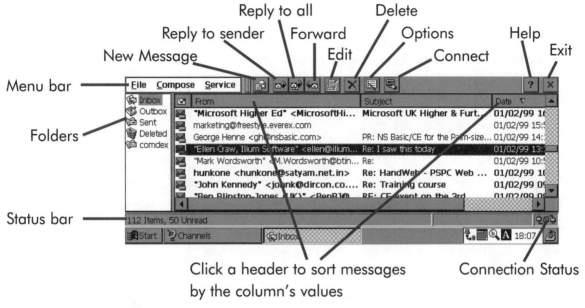

Reply to all · Delete

Reply to sender · Forward · Options · Help

New Message · Edit · Connect · Exit

Menu bar

Folders

Status bar

Click a header to sort messages by the column's values

Connection Status

Inbox on the H/PC Professional Edition

Send/Receive E-mail

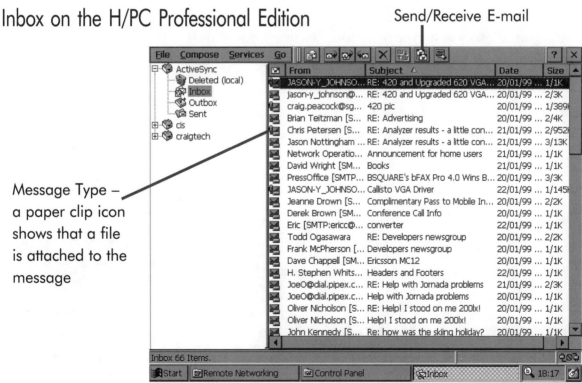

Message Type – a paper clip icon shows that a file is attached to the message

Inbox on the H/PC Pro – new features

The latest version of Inbox adds support for IMAP4 servers. Used in conjunction with LDAP, this can save time when composing and managing e-mails. Corporate e-mail servers such as Microsoft Exchange Server support the IMAP4 protocol and also LDAP. I'll briefly mention these, but in the examples I'm going to show POP3 support, the most commonly used e-mail protocol on the Internet.

IMAP4 has many features including the ability to allow you to browse your messages directly on the server without having to download the entire mailbox first.

IMAP4 and Inbox's support of offline folders means you can organize your files on your Handheld PC Pro, and when you next link to your PC, the messages will be stored in folders with the same names on your PC.

LDAP, when running on a suitable server (such as Microsoft Exchange), allows you to type in a person's name when composing a message. It then looks up the address of the recipient.

Over the next few pages you will set up one connection for Internet e-mail and look at another connection for transferring e-mails from the desktop. You are not limited to having just two e-mail services, some people have four or five.

Jargon

POP3 – Post Office Protocol 3, for receiving e-mail.

SMTP – Simple Mail Transport Protocol, for sending e-mail.

IMAP4 – Internet Message Access Protocol version 4, for retrieving e-mail.

LDAP – Lightweight Directory Access Protocol, for looking up e-mail addresses.

Service – The name given when you set up Inbox for a connection.

Tip

In the latest version on the Handheld PC Pro, links to Web sites are underlined in e-mails. If you double-tap on one, Pocket Internet Explorer will run and, if you are online, you will be taken to the site.

Take note

On CE 2.0 devices the service name for transferring messages from your PC is Windows CE Inbox Services. On newer versions, it's referred to as ActiveSync.

Basic steps

1 Open up Inbox.

2 Tap Services – Options....

3 On the Services panel, tap Add.

4 Highlight Internet E-mail and tap OK.

5 Give the service a name – most people use the name of their service provider.

6 Tap OK.

Setting up your Inbox

You'll need several key pieces of information before you can set up and test your e-mail connection. If you don't have this information on hand give your Internet service provider a call – their technical support department should be able to help.

● Your e-mail address.

● Your e-mail login name and password.

● The name of your Internet provider's e-mail server which you will use to receive e-mail – normally the POP3 host or POP3 e-mail server, though it is possible for your Internet provider to support IMAP4.

● The name of your Internet provider's server for sending e-mail, known as the SMTP server. Some providers use different servers for sending and receiving e-mails.

You must have a working modem and connection to your Internet provider to test this next section.

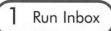

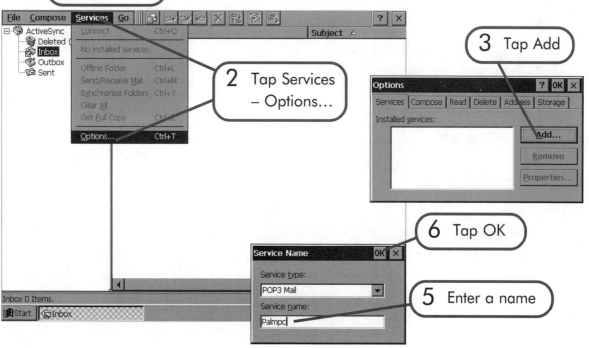

Defining the service

This takes time, but only needs doing once for each service.

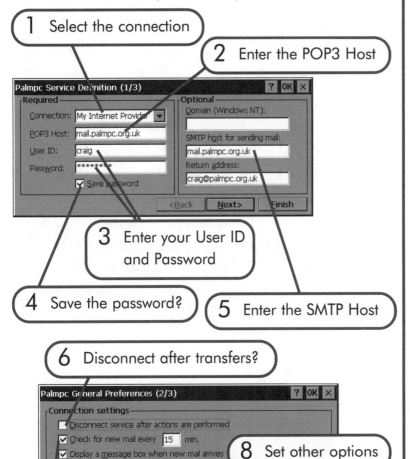

1. Select the connection

2. Enter the POP3 Host

Palmpc Service Definition (1/3)   ? OK ✕

Required
- Connection: My Internet Provider ▼
- POP3 Host: mail.palmpc.org.uk
- User ID: craig
- Password: ********
- ☑ Save password

Optional
- Domain (Windows NT):
- SMTP host for sending mail: mail.palmpc.org.uk
- Return address: craig@palmpc.org.uk

<Back   Next>   Finish

3. Enter your User ID and Password

4. Save the password?

5. Enter the SMTP Host

6. Disconnect after transfers?

Palmpc General Preferences (2/3)   ? OK ✕

Connection settings
- ☐ Disconnect service after actions are performed
- ☑ Check for new mail every 15 min.
- ☑ Display a message box when new mail arrives
- ☑ Send using MIME format
- ☑ Only display messages from the last 3 days

<Back   Next>   Finish

8. Set other options

7. Check for mail while online?

Basic steps

1. Open the Connection drop-down list and select your new one.

2. Enter your POP3 host.

3. Enter your User ID and Password.

4. Tick Save Password if you don't want to have to enter it every time you connect.

5. Enter your SMTP Host – usually the same for sending and receiving – and tap Next.

6. Tick Disconnect service... to hang up after getting your new mail.

7. Check Check for new e-mail every *X* minutes when connected if you are often online for long periods of time.

Take note

Inbox will generate a **Return Address** in the form "userid@pop3host." If yours does not follow this pattern, write it into the field on the first panel.

8 Set the other options to suit yourself and tap Next.

9 Set the On Connect option and tap Finish.

Tip

Even if you have Message headers only, then you can still download the entire message with attachments on a per e-mail basis.

Message headers only – shows the sender, date and subject

100 lines will get the whole of most messages, though if there is an attached file, you may have to download it again later.

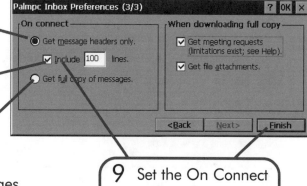

Palmpc Inbox Preferences (3/3)   ? OK ×

On connect
◉ Get message headers only.
☑ Include 100 lines.
○ Get full copy of messages.

When downloading full copy
☑ Get meeting requests (limitations exist; see Help).
☑ Get file attachments.

<Back   Next>   Finish

Download the full copy of all messages

9 Set the On Connect option and finish

Take note

Inbox has a set of options to define how to manage, store and delete your messages. Leave these at their defaults until you have been using Inbox for a little while. You will then have a better idea of how you want to manage your e-mail.

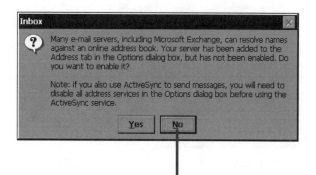

Inbox   ×

? Many e-mail servers, including Microsoft Exchange, can resolve names against an online address book. Your server has been added to the Address tab in the Options dialog box, but has not been enabled. Do you want to enable it?

Note: if you also use ActiveSync to send messages, you will need to disable all address services in the Options dialog box before using the ActiveSync service.

Yes   No

If you are only using the Internet e-mail, select No at this dialog box – the feature is mainly used on corporate e-mail servers

Getting your e-mail

To actually make the connection to your Internet provider you will first need to plug in your modem and make sure it is connected to a phone line. Some modems drain the batteries of your Handheld PC really quickly. It is therefore recommended that you use an AC adapter when working online.

1 Tap Service – Connect or tap 🔲 the Connect icon.

or

2 If you are already connected, tap 🔳 the Send/Receive icon.

3 Status Messages should appear and the disconnected/ connected icon will change.

4 Your new messages should appear in Inbox.

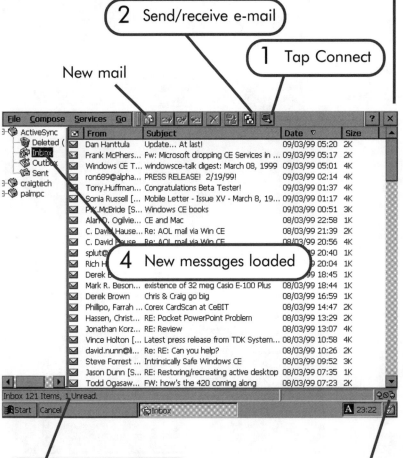

2 Send/receive e-mail

1 Tap Connect

New mail

4 New messages loaded

3 Watch the Status bar   Connected/Disconnected icon

Basic steps

1 Tap the New Mail icon.

2 In the To field, enter the e-mail address of the person you are sending e-mail to.

or

3 If the person's e-mail address is in the Contacts application, enter the first letter of their name (either first or last) and tap the Address Book icon.

4 Select the person from the list that appears.

5 Type your message.

6 Tap the Send mail icon. If you are not online the message will be transferred to the Outbox folder for sending later.

Send/Receive mail

When you connect up to your Internet provider your outbound e-mail is automatically sent and messages waiting for you are received. If you have been connected for a while and wish to send/receive e-mail then you can press [Ctrl] + [M] or tap Services – Send/Receive mail. On the newest Windows CE machines there is a Send/Receive icon.

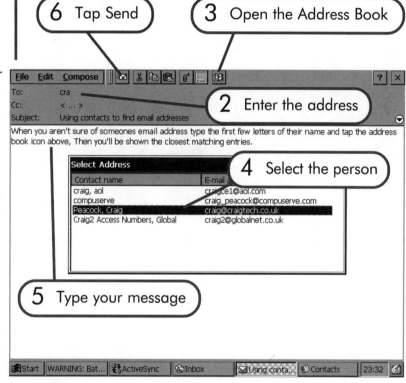

- 6 Tap Send
- 3 Open the Address Book
- 2 Enter the address
- 4 Select the person
- 5 Type your message

Tip

To save typing in e-mail addresses, use the Address Book.

E-mail attachments

Handling e-mail attachments is another one of those areas that has seen great improvements over recent years. The latest versions of Windows CE have the ability to open up documents that have been created in the Microsoft desktop applications such as Word or Excel 97.

On versions of Windows CE before 2.1 it was not possible to open up a Microsoft Word 97 or Excel 97 document on the Windows CE mobile device unless this document had been saved in a special way, but now it is quite straightforward.

Basic steps

1 On the Handheld PC Pro, double-tap on the attachment filename at the bottom of the screen.

2 On the Handheld PR, tap the paper clip to reveal the attachment.

3 Select the attached file – there may be more than one.

4 Tap OK.

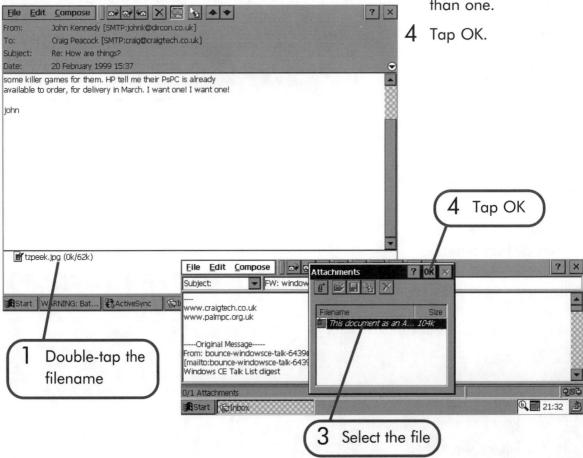

4 Tap OK

1 Double-tap the filename

3 Select the file

1 Open the e-mail from your new contact.

2 Tap Compose.

3 Tap Add Sender to Contacts....

4 Follow the steps on page 40 to add any other details about your new contact.

❏ When you have finished you are returned to the e-mail that you were in.

With Windows CE 2.1 onwards, mobile device users can take advantage of a new feature to carry out one of the commonest e-mail tasks – adding a contact's details. **Add Sender to Contacts** saves lots of time and avoids the problem of mistyping an e-mail address.

You can add the sender's details at any point when you are reading an e-mail.

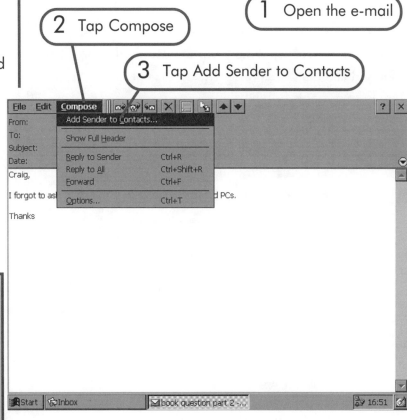

Take note
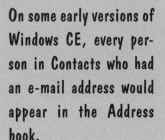

On some early versions of Windows CE, every person in Contacts who had an e-mail address would appear in the Address book.

E-mail signatures

A feature still missing from the Windows CE system is e-mail signatures. While this is a luxury to some users it drives others crazy (judging by the number of e-mails I get about the topic!).

There are a couple of third-party utilities that solve this problem, there may well be more available soon.

Landware's QuickText, with its easy-to-use options and interface, has been designed to make entering text quick and easy. An e-mail signature is no problem for this little application. After loading, it sits nicely on the taskbar — just a tap away whenever you need it.

To use QuickText you simply tap the menu entry when it is displayed and the text gets inserted in the current application. Here is an example in Inbox.

Basic steps

1 Double-tap **A** the QuickText icon.

❑ Creating QuickText

2 Tap Edit if you want to create a new entry.

3 Tap New.

4 Give your entry a name and enter the text and tap OK.

❑ Using QuickText

5 Place the cursor where you want the text.

6 Tap **A**.

7 Tap an entry to select it and write it into your message.

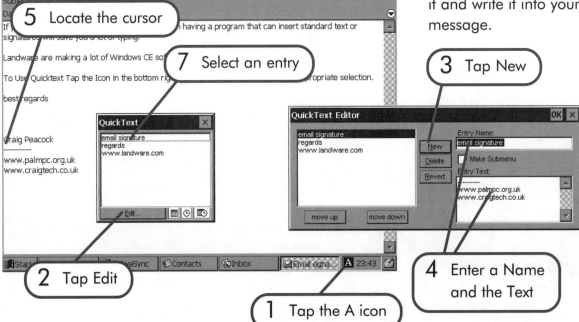

116

Folders in Inbox

Basic steps

1 Tap the Inbox folder.
2 Tap File.
3 Tap Folder.
4 Tap New Folder.
5 Give the folder a name .
6 Tap OK.

If you find yourself managing a large number of e-mails then the best way to do this is by creating folders. Once you have created folders you can move or copy your messages to them from the Inbox folder.

You will need to create folders under an existing folder, so let's create a folder under Inbox called "Important."

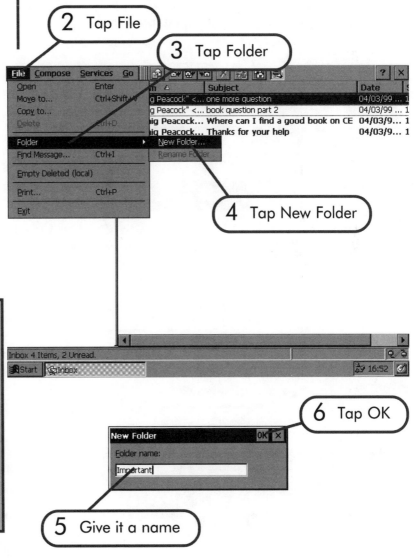

2 Tap File

3 Tap Folder

4 Tap New Folder

5 Give it a name

6 Tap OK

Tip

If you see a plus sign beside a folder name, then there are folders within the one you have selected. Tap once on the plus sign to reveal them.

Copying and moving messages

Messages can be copied or moved between folders — try it with your new folder. After copying some, tap the new folder in the left-hand view to check that they are there.

When you try to move a message from Inbox to a folder you get a warning message. Take care! As the dialog box says, if you move a message and you've only downloaded part of it, you won't be able to get the rest of the message from your Windows CE device. However, it will come through correctly on a PC.

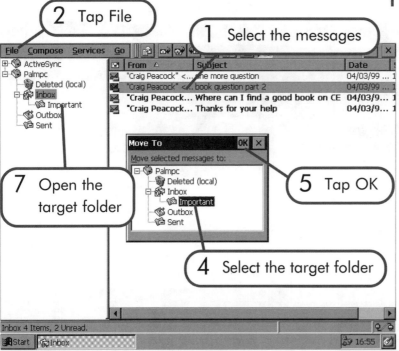

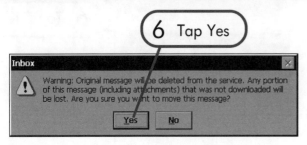

Basic steps

1 Select one or more messages – to select several hold down [Ctrl] and tap each message in turn.

2 Tap File.

3 Tap Copy To or Move To.

4 Select the target folder – tap the plus sign to reach folders within a folder.

5 Tap OK.

6 When moving messages, you may get a warning at the end, tap Yes to confirm the move.

7 Tap the target folder to see its contents.

Take note

On Windows CE 1.x and 2.0 you do not get a warning message when moving messages, so take extra care.

118

Basic steps

❑ Setting up a service

1 Tap Compose.

2 Tap Option.

3 Tap Service.

4 Tap Add.

5 Follow the instructions from the earlier section (page 109).

Take note

Not all Palm-size PCs are equipped with modems. You may need to check with your hardware vendor.

Inbox on Palm-size PCs

As with most other Microsoft Windows CE applications Inbox on the Palm-size PC functions identically to the Handheld PC version, but looks a little different because of the screen size.

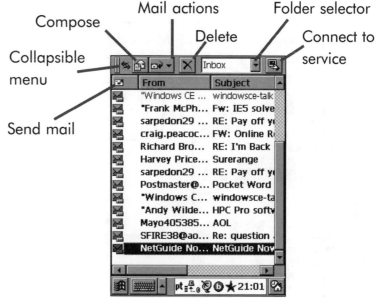

Compose — Mail actions — Folder selector — Delete — Connect to service — Collapsible menu — Send mail

Creating a new e-mail service

Setting up e-mail on a Palm-size PC is exactly the same as on the Handheld PC. Before you set up a service on your Palm-size PC, you should ensure you have a working dial-up connection to your Internet provider, see *Setting up your Inbox* (page 109).

The Options panel for a service – these are best set after you have used e-mail for a while, and know more about how you want to manage your e-mail

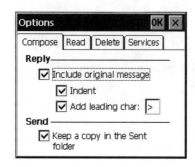

119

Responding to e-mails

When responding to an e-mail on the Palm-size PC you can select whether you wish to reply to sender, reply to all or forward the message. The options are all reached through the drop-down menu on the Mail Actions button.

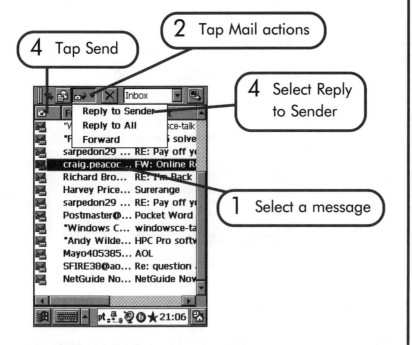

Basic steps

1 Highlight a message you wish to reply to.

2 Tap the Mail actions button.

3 Select Reply to Sender.

4 The Message will be opened up and you can type your reply.

5 If you want to send attachments or copy and paste the e-mail text, tap the collapsible menu bar.

6 Tap Send e-mail when you are done. If you are offline, the message will be stored in Outbox for sending later.

Take note

You can e-mail people from Contacts. When you have a contact's name highlighted in Contacts, tap the Create message icon. Pocket Inbox will then open, ready for you to compose a message to that person.

On the Handheld PC, if you highlight multiple recipients in Contacts (by holding down [Ctrl] and tapping on each one you want to select) and then tap the Create Message icon, all the people in your list will be added to the To: field in the create a new message part of Inbox.

Basic steps

❑ Creating a folder

1 Open the collapsible menu and tap File.

2 Tap Folder.

3 Tap New Folder.

4 Give your folder a name.

5 Tap OK.

6 Tap the collapsible menu icon again to return to the main graphical view.

7 Tap the drop-down box to the right of Inbox to reveal all the folders.

8 Tap a folder to open it.

or

9 Tap the drop-down box a second time to stay in the same Inbox folder.

Inbox folders

Folders on the Palm-size PC work in the same way as on the Handheld PC. You can copy and move messages to them and use them to organize your messages.

It's simple to create new folders and to move between your folders.

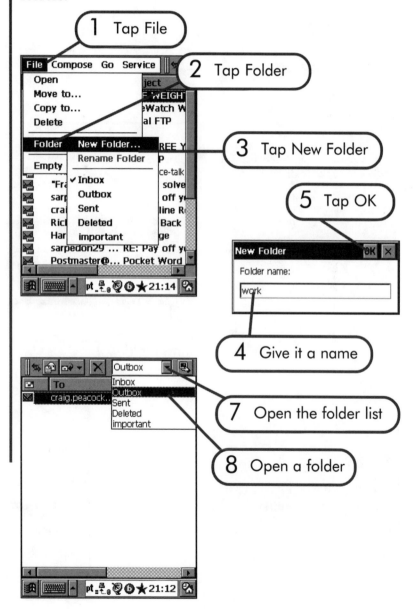

Moving and copying messages

In this example I will show you how to copy a message to a folder.

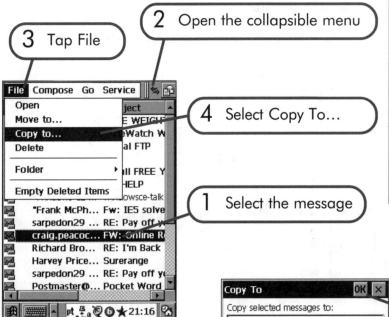

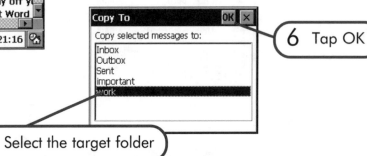

2 Open the collapsible menu

3 Tap File

4 Select Copy To...

1 Select the message

6 Tap OK

5 Select the target folder

1 Highlight a message by tapping on it once.

2 Tap the collapsible menu icon.

3 Tap File.

4 Tap Copy To....

5 Select the folder you wish to copy the message to.

6 Tap OK.

Tip

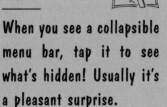

When you see a collapsible menu bar, tap it to see what's hidden! Usually it's a pleasant surprise.

Take note

Moving, copying and deleting messages only affect those in your mobile device. The messages will be retained in full when you connect to your Internet provider to download your e-mail from your PC.

Basic steps

❏ To create a signature

1 Tap 🐾 the PalmSquirt Text icon.

2 Tap Edit.

3 Give your entry a name and type the text.

4 Tap New to save the entry.

❏ Using a signature

5 Type your message.

6 Tap 🐾 the PalmSquirt Text icon.

7 Tap the appropriate entry and the text is put into the e-mail.

There are several products available from third-party vendors that help save time when using Palm-size PCs. One such product is from *The Unsupported Software Company*. It's called PalmSquirtText and it allows you to store commonly used text and insert it into documents. One handy use for it is to create a signature to add to the end of your e-mails. Here's how.

Notice the icon on the Taskbar. This shows that PalmSquirtText is running — I started it earlier from my Start Menu.

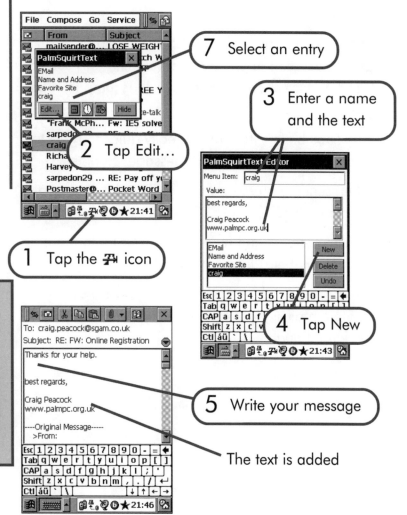

7 Select an entry

3 Enter a name and the text

2 Tap Edit...

1 Tap the 🐾 icon

4 Tap New

5 Write your message

The text is added

Tip

The Unsupported Software Company has released over 100 Freeware titles for Windows CE Palm-size PCs.

Summary

- ❏ E-mail looks different on all three types of Windows CE devices.

- ❏ You may need to ask your Internet provider for the names of their mail servers when setting up e-mail.

- ❏ You can create messages offline and send them when you next connect up to the Internet.

- ❏ When you collect e-mail on a mobile device, you only pick up a copy from the server – the original remains there.

- ❏ With Inbox on the Windows CE Handheld PC Pro devices you can open up e-mail attachments such as Word and Excel documents as well as jump to Web sites.

- ❏ Inbox has buttons to make it really quick to reply to incoming mail and forward messages to others.

- ❏ When sending messages you can send it to several people at once.

- ❏ Creating folders and moving messages into these new folders helps tidy up your Inbox.

- ❏ Using some third-party software it's possible to create e-mail signatures – try not to make signatures too long though.

9 Other applications

Travel with Windows CE

When you travel you want to take lots of information with you but you also want to carry as little possible. Windows CE and various third-party applications can help you out on this front as well. This chapter will show you some third-party software that has maps to help you find your way around and even applications to keep your data organized and even password protected. You will also see how to set up your visiting city and create appointments for the country you are visiting.

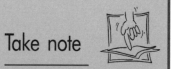

Take note

This screenshot is from an H/PC Pro, but Pocket Streets is also available on the H/PCs and Palm-size PCs.

Microsoft Pocket Streets

If you buy a copy of AutoRoute Express GB 2000 or install Expedia Streets from the CD-ROM, then you can create your own maps with points of interest and export them to your mobile device and access them when you are traveling.

Find place   Up/Down Left/Right   Pushpin – used to create

Menu bar   Zoom in/out   custom areas on the maps

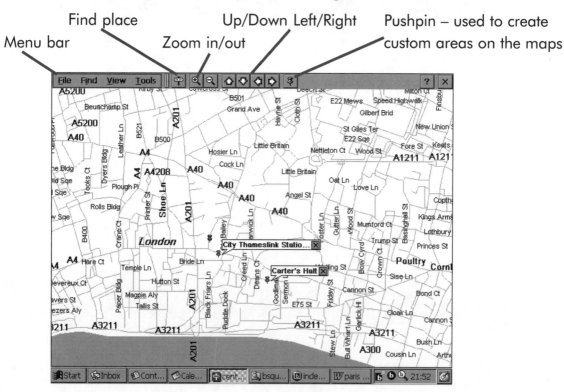

World Travel Companion

On board info has taken the extremely popular AA City Pack Travel Guides and made them available on Windows CE. The guides are packed with features and even include details on major festivals throughout the year.

Here are the main features of the product.

1   Background on the city and its inhabitants;

2   How to organize your time (itineraries from a single evening to a full day);

3   Top 25 sights;

4   Where to eat, shop, be entertained, stay;

5   Travel facts, practical information and useful phrases.

The electronic versions of these travel companions cover around 80% of their printed counterparts, only the maps and photos are missing.

The travel facts show not only hours of service, but costs of typical journeys and phone numbers of the bus and train companies.

You can choose to install as few or as many of the cities as you wish. The information is displayed using Microsoft Pocket Internet Explorer on your Handheld PC and navigating around is just like navigating around Internet sites.

Tip

If you install your chosen city from the World Travel Companion and also install the city from Microsoft Pocket Streets, you'll have the guide and the map on your device.

Take note

Games go mobile! The good news is there are more games available for Windows CE than any other type of application, the bad news is I haven't room to cover them in this book. But then, learning to play is half the fun of many games!

World Clock

Using World Clock alongside Calendar can help you to create appointments all around the world. You can get your mobile device to do all the work of making sure your meetings are all scheduled at the correct time and in the correct time zone.

The World Clock is found in several places on your Windows CE device. The quickest way to launch it is to double-tap on the clock in the lower right-hand corner of the screen.

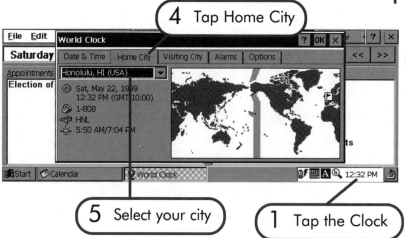

4 Tap Home City

5 Select your city

1 Tap the Clock

When you've selected your home city you will have several items of information and some new icons on the screen.

- Date and time (and what time zone and offset from GMT your home city is in).

- Country and telephone area code.

- Main Airport and its identifying 3 characters (e.g. LHR = London Heathrow).

- Time of dawn and dusk.

- When you have the visiting city displayed you will also see the distance it is from your home city.

- On the map you will see 🏠 representing your home city, and 🏳 representing the visiting city.

Basic steps

1 Double-tap the Clock.

or

2 Tap Start – Settings – Control Panel and select World Clock.

or

3 Tap Start and open the World Clock from the Accessories menu.

❑ To set your home city

4 Tap the Home City tab.

5 Tap the drop-down arrow and scroll down to find your closest city or type in the first letter or two of its name.

Tip

Whether you have your Home or Visiting city highlighted will depend on which icon flashes on the map.

Basic steps

❏ Setting the visiting city

1 Tap the Visiting City tab.

2 Select a city.

3 Tap OK.

❏ To swap between cities

4 Tap the button to the left of the name of the visiting city.

5 Tap OK. Your time will now have changed as if you were in your visiting city.

6 Start Calendar and create the appointments for your visit.

❏ To get back to the local time, repeat the process changing back to the home city.

Changing the Visiting City

To change the visiting city you use the same process as for the home city, but you will see some extra information displayed.

You are about to go on a trip to a foreign country and you want to make sure all your meetings are in your mobile device and that you won't have to figure out the time zone differences. Here is how to create meetings in a different country/city.

When you wish to create a meeting in the visiting city you must first swap to it. Then you can create the appointment in the normal way. When you get to your destination you should change your settings to be those of the visiting city and then your appointments will all be in the correct time zone!

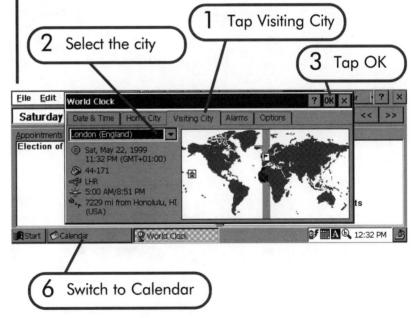

Pocket PowerPoint

On the Handheld PC and the Handheld PC Pro machines you will find Pocket PowerPoint, which allows you to display PowerPoint presentations that have been created on your PC. Some mobile devices come equipped with a VGA-out port, which you can use to display presentations on a monitor or a large screen via a suitable projector.

You can customize a presentation on the device, for example, changing the Title slide, modifying slide notes, and hiding slides.

As you cannot create presentations on the device you will need to transfer them to your device from your PC.

❑ To open a presentation

1 Launch Pocket PowerPoint from a desktop icon or from the Start menu.

2 Select the presentation you want to open.

3 Tap OK.

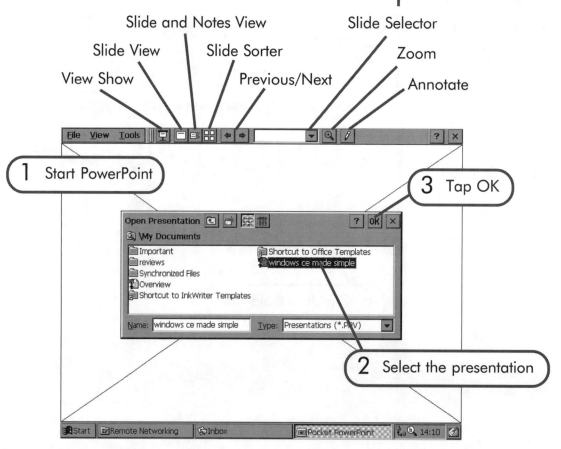

Slide and Notes View

Slide View   Slide Sorter

View Show   Previous/Next

Slide Selector

Zoom

Annotate

1 Start PowerPoint

3 Tap OK

2 Select the presentation

130

Basic steps

1 Tap the Tools menu then tap Title Slide.

2 Enter the details you want on the title slide.

3 It is possible to change the Font and Position of the text on the title slide – just tap the buttons and experiment with the different settings.

4 Tap the Preview button to view the effect of your changes.

5 Tap OK when you have finished editing the slide.

Creating a new Title Screen

It is possible to create a new title screen on the device. This means that you may customize your presentation without having to transfer a different version from your PC every time you want to just change the title.

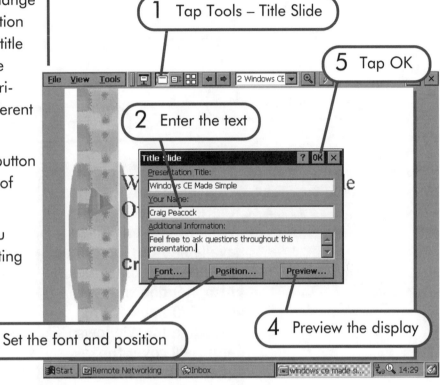

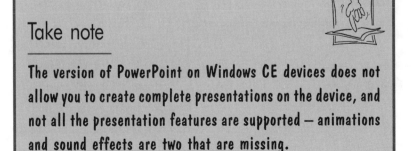

Take note

The version of PowerPoint on Windows CE devices does not allow you to create complete presentations on the device, and not all the presentation features are supported – animations and sound effects are two that are missing.

Using Slide Notes

Slide notes are used to enable you to prompt yourself about the slide that is being displayed. They are not available when displaying a presentation on the built-in screen but they are viewable when using an external device such as a monitor or projector.

Here is how you can edit the slide notes on your device and increase the font size to make viewing them easier.

1 Select the slide from the drop-down list.

2 Tap into the notes box and start typing.

3 Tap the font size icon to increase the size of the text.

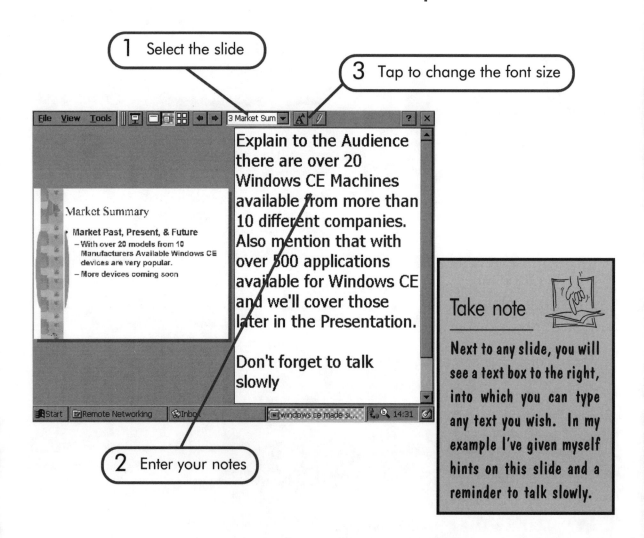

1 Select the slide

3 Tap to change the font size

Explain to the Audience there are over 20 Windows CE Machines available from more than 10 different companies. Also mention that with over 500 applications available for Windows CE and we'll cover those later in the Presentation.

Don't forget to talk slowly

Market Summary

Market Past, Present, & Future
– With over 20 models from 10 Manufacturers Available Windows CE devices are very popular.
– More devices coming soon

2 Enter your notes

Take note

Next to any slide, you will see a text box to the right, into which you can type any text you wish. In my example I've given myself hints on this slide and a reminder to talk slowly.

Hiding and moving slides

1 Tap the Slide Sorter
icon.

2 Scroll up or down
through the list and
select the slide you
want to hide or move.

❏ Hiding a slide

3 Tap the Hide Slide
check box to tick it.

Note – the numbers
change depending on
your selection.

❏ Moving a slide

4 Tap the Up/Down
arrows to nudge the
slide into its new
position.

5 Tap OK when you
have finished moving
or hiding slides.

It is possible to hide slides with Pocket PowerPoint and that's
done in the Slide Sorter view. You can also reorder your slides
in this screen.

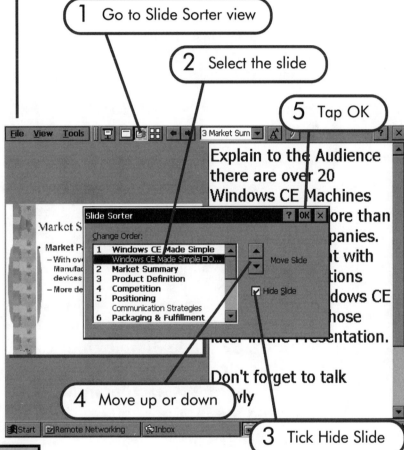

1 Go to Slide Sorter view

2 Select the slide

5 Tap OK

4 Move up or down

3 Tick Hide Slide

Tip

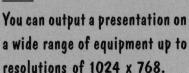

**You can output a presentation on
a wide range of equipment up to
resolutions of 1024 x 768.**

Showing the presentation

To run your presentation, tap the View Show icon. If you view your presentation on the Internal display then you will see four icons on the top right of the display.

Once you are running your presentation you can experiment with the Annotate option, which allows you to draw on the screen to highlight certain features to your audience.

Setting up for an external device

If you wish to have your presentation automatically advance every x seconds or manually control the output then you need to change the options in Set Up Show.

Basic steps

1 Tap Tools.

2 Tap Set up Show.

3 Select the drop-down box and pick your required output mode.

4 If you wish to have your presentation advance automatically between slides select it here and enter the time in seconds.

Show Presentation / Return to Edit mode

Product Definition

- **Windows CE Made Simple offers readers a simple way of getting the most of out of this exciting new operating system**
- **Covers Microsoft Windows CE on Handheld PCs (H/PC) and Palm-size PCs (PSPC)**

2/20/99

Back a slide

Forward a slide

Annotate slide

Tip

To manually move between slides use the cursor keys.

To edit it again, tap the Show Presentation/Return to edit mode icon.

134

Spreadsheets

There is no spreadsheet application supplied as standard on the Palm-size PC, but a couple of companies have written spreadsheet applications for these devices.

● **BSQUARE** with their BSQUARE spreadsheet application.

● **Surerange Analysis** with their Pocket Sheet product.

BSQUARE Development has a spreadsheet product available for palm-size devices; it is compatible with Microsoft Excel and allows you to edit and perform calculations, etc. on the device.

The BSQUARE spreadsheet can be used for data storage as well as for calculations – here it is being used to hold a set of Internet addresses

Please check out the relevant companies' Web sites for more details on their products.

BSQUARE at http://www.bsquare.com

Surerange Analysis at http://www.surerange.com

Voice Recorder

This amazingly handy application is available on all Palm-size as well some Handheld PCs. You can make approximately 1 hour of recordings and only take up 1Mb of space.

Most Palm-size PCs have hardware buttons to activate features of the Voice Recorder application. You can press and hold the record button on all machines (even if it is switched off). It will switch the machine on if required, open up the voice recorder application and start recording. To stop recording, let go of the button – you then will find yourself in the Voice Recorder. You may then want to change the name from the default *RecordingX*.

Basic steps

❑ To rename a recording

1 Select the recording.

2 Tap the Properties icon.

or

3 Use the File – Rename command.

4 Change the name to something more meaningful.

5 Tap OK.

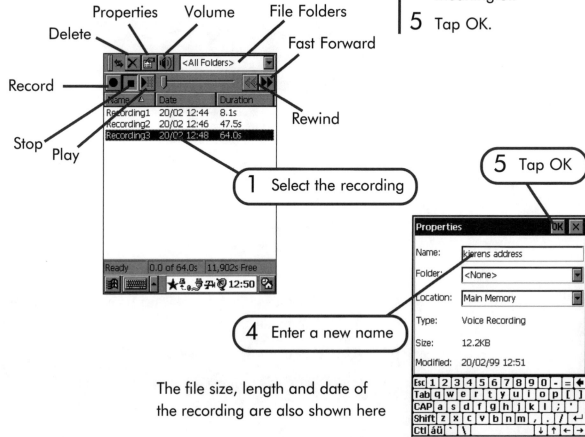

The file size, length and date of the recording are also shown here

Basic steps

1 Tap Tools then tap Recording Format.

2 Change the format to PCM.

3 Select the quality of sound required. The 8,000 Hz, 8 Bit Mono (8KB/s) is usually best. This is compatible with more computers but produces much larger files than their mobile voice equivalents.

4 Tap OK.

File formats

If you are sending voice recordings to people who do not have a Palm-size PC, then before you make the recording you need to change the file format from its default (Mobile Voice) to PCM – here's how to do it.

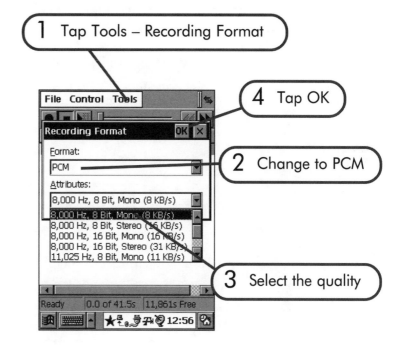

1 Tap Tools – Recording Format

4 Tap OK

2 Change to PCM

3 Select the quality

File Control Tools

Recording Format   OK ✕

Format:
PCM

Attributes:
8,000 Hz, 8 Bit, Mono (8 KB/s)
8,000 Hz, 8 Bit, Mono, (8 KB/s)
8,000 Hz, 8 Bit, Stereo (16 KB/s)
8,000 Hz, 16 Bit, Mono (16 KB/s)
8,000 Hz, 16 Bit, Stereo (31 KB/s)
11,025 Hz, 8 Bit, Mono (11 KB/s)

Ready   0.0 of 41.5s   11,861s Free
12:56

Take note

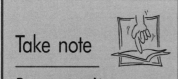

Better quality means larger files – the KB/s value is the one to watch, the higher the figure, the better the quality.

File **Control** Tools
Play   ●
Sequential Play
Pause   ●
Stop   ○
Record New   🎙
Fast Playback   Hold⟳

Ready   0.0 of 41.5s   11,861s Free
12:54

The icons on the Control menu correspond to those printed near the actual buttons on the case of your Palm-size PC

Sending files to devices

You can exchange information between devices by e-mail or infrared. Here I am sending a file from a Palm-size via infrared, using a Handheld PC to receive the file.

Files can also be sent to an e-mail recipient, and you can do this from within the file, rather than attaching it while composing an e-mail message.

The File – Send To command is present in all the main Windows CE applications on the Palm-size PC – this screen shot is taken from the Voice Recorder.

- Using infrared

1 Highlight file or entry you wish to send.

2 The recipient must tap File – Receive.

3 Tap File.

4 Tap Send To.

5 Tap Infrared Recipient.

6 Line up the devices. The file will be transmitted – wait for the *"file successfully sent"* message.

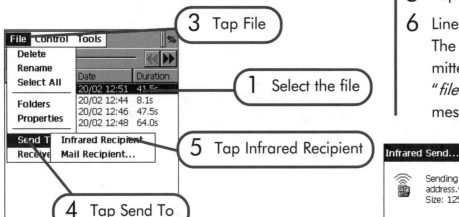

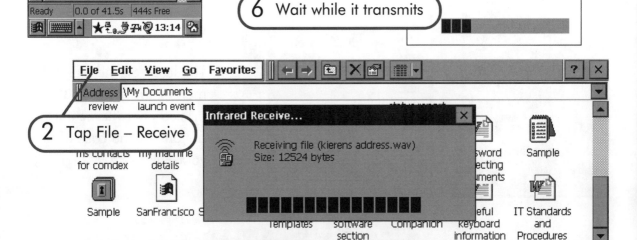

138

Basic steps

1 Double-tap the bFIND icon to launch it.

2 Enter the text you are looking for.

3 Tap to tick the check boxes for those areas that you want to search.

4 To narrow your search down to a particular folder, tap the Browse button underneath the Look In Folder field to find the one you want.

5 Tap the Search button.

BSQUARE Development Corporation has created a program called bFIND which some Windows CE vendors have included with their mobile devices. Here is a quick overview of how to use bFIND to locate information on your device.

bFIND allows you to search lots of different types of data to help you find what you are searching for, it includes the ability to search for filenames, phrases and even single word occurrences.

With bFIND you don't have to be in any application to start your search, you double-tap the icon on the taskbar. bFIND then searches documents, spreadsheets, e-mail, contacts, Pocket Word and Pocket Excel and even other databases to help you find that piece of information.

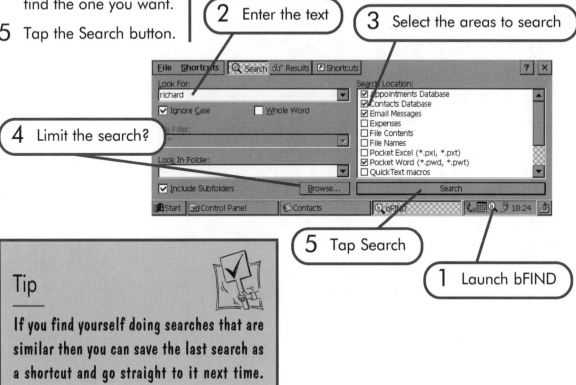

2 Enter the text

3 Select the areas to search

4 Limit the search?

5 Tap Search

1 Launch bFIND

Tip

If you find yourself doing searches that are similar then you can save the last search as a shortcut and go straight to it next time.

Summary

❑ Microsoft Pocket Streets is the mobile partner of AutoRoute Express GB 2000 and Expedia Streets and lets you copy parts of maps to your device.

❑ The World Travel Companion features backgrounds on cities, places to eat and drink as well as stay!

❑ World Clock lets you keep track of times and other useful information for your Home and Visiting cities.

❑ With Pocket PowerPoint you can run and edit presentations on your mobile device.

❑ Creating a personalized title slide for your audience can make a big difference.

❑ You can create slide notes and hide slides of a PowerPoint presentation on your mobile device.

❑ BSQUARE and SureRange Analysis have released spreadsheet applications for Palm-size devices.

❑ Most Windows CE devices have a built-in Voice Recorder, which you can use to record quick notes and play them back or e-mail them to others.

❑ When sending Voice recordings to others you might have to change the format.

❑ All Windows CE devices have an Infrared port which can be used to exchange information, contacts, voice recordings with other Windows CE users.

❑ When you are hunting for a particular appointment, letter or even e-mail with a certain phrase in it, bFind will find it quickly.

Web sites

My Windows CE site, with links to over 500 vendors' sites.
http://www.craigtech.co.uk

My Palm-size PC Web site
http://www.palmpc.org.uk

Vendors

Anyware Consulting
(http://hometown.aol.com/anyware)

Applian Software
http://www.applian.com

bSquare
http://www.bsquare.com

CIC
http://www.cic.com

DeveloperOne
http://www.developerone.com

Ilium Software
http://www.iliumsoft.com

Kensai Design Windows CE pages
http://windowsce.kensai.com

Landware
http:// www.landware.com

Microsoft Windows CE
http://www.microsoft.com/windowsce/default.asp

Sticky Software
http://www.sticky.co.uk

Surerange Analysis
http://www.surerange.com

Magazines

Handheld PC Magazine
http://www.hpcmag.com

PC Plus Magazine
http://www.pcplus.co.uk

Pen Computing Magazine
http://www.pencomputing.com

WindowsCEPower Magazine
http://www.windowscepower.com

Special interest

Handheld PC Development Checklist
http://www.microsoft.com/windowsce/pccompanions/developer/hpctools.asp

Microsoft MSN
http://www.computingcentral.msn.com

Mike's Palm-size PC Web Site – Lots of great and free software for Palm-size PCs.
http://www.homestead.com/palm/

Todd's Windows CE Compendium
http://www.to-tech.com

WinCEbiz
http://www.wincebiz.com

Index